To Barbara Tapping:
Thank you for your support.
Al & Elizabeth

CONSTITUTIONAL HIRING & FIRING THE PRESIDENT

CONSTITUTIONAL
HIRING & FIRING THE
PRESIDENT

—

SYSTEM OPERATIONS MANUAL

Albert W. Small, Ph.D

Elizabeth A. Downey-Small

Downey & Small Associates, Inc.
System Operations Analysis and Publishing

D&S™

Downey & Small Associates, Inc.
System Operations Analysis and Publishing
Kensington, Maryland, U.S.A.
SystemOps@DowneySmall.com™.

Printed in the United States of America

2017 16 15 14 13 11 10 9 8 7 6

ISBN10: 0-9764580-3-9
ISBN13: 978-0-9764580-3-6

D&S™ SystemOps™ Manual, DS-SOM-CHFP-v.1.6

Downey & Small Associates, Inc. has provided Management Consulting and System Engineering services since its incorporation in 1981, and began System Operations Analysis and Publishing activities in 2001.

Dedicated to America's Patriots
who gave us Liberty and defended our Constitution,

With Gratitude for their Sacrifices.

Soli Deo Gloria.

Contents

Diagrams

Tables

Preface

Constitutional hiring and firing the President of the United States of America can be complex. Citizens should know how the U.S. Constitution addresses various situations. This manual is intended to help people understand the Constitution's provisions and be prepared for unexpected circumstances and outcomes during election, installation, and removal of the President.

Citizens are more likely to accept results unpleasing to them if they can see the legitimacy of the process followed. And, they will be able to detect illegitimate processes and take appropriate action.

This System Operations Manual provides a graphic description of the process for employing and dismissing a President, and includes Constitution cross reference tables. The manual emphasizes the Constitution's requirements, and includes information from some relevant laws enacted in accordance with the Constitution.

American patriots throughout history have given their lives to defend our Constitution. It falls upon us now to require our civilian officials honor their oaths to the Constitution.

I.

Introduction

We the People of the United States, in Order to form a more perfect Union, establish Justice, insure domestic Tranquility, provide for the common defense, promote the general Welfare, and secure the Blessings of Liberty to ourselves and our Posterity, do ordain and establish this Constitution for the United States of America.

Constitution Preamble

We the People

"We the People" have the right and civic duty to know how our Constitutional system is designed to function, and what must be done when it does not serve the purpose of government defined in the self-evident truths of America's national charter, the Declaration of Independence.[1]

> We hold these truths to be self-evident, that all men are created equal, that they are endowed by their Creator with certain unalienable Rights, that among these are Life, Liberty and the pursuit of Happiness.--
>
> That to secure these rights, Governments are instituted among Men, deriving their just powers from the consent of the governed,--
>
> That whenever any Form of Government becomes destructive of these ends, it is the Right of the People to alter or to abolish it, and to institute new Government, laying its foundation on such principles and organizing its powers in such form, as to them shall seem most likely to effect their Safety and Happiness. …

Self-evident truths, by definition, are immutable and transcend governments and laws for all time.[2]

The Declaration specifies that the People—not legislators, not executives, and not judges—retain the right to evaluate the performance of government, and take the action they deem appropriate if they judge it failing its purpose.

The Constitution is America's third form of government, following King George III's tyranny and the weak Articles of Confederation, both of which failed to meet the criteria of the Declaration. The Constitution provides for its own amendment by agreement of three-fourths of the States, and has remained our form of government through 27 amendments over two centuries.

Since government derives its "just powers from the consent of the governed," the People have the right and duty to ensure government remains within the bounds they set. When the People abdicate, government becomes their master.

The People should continuously evaluate the supreme Law of the Land[3]—Constitution, Laws and Treaties—to ensure it is "Declarational," and the Laws and Treaties are Constitutional. We have full authority and sufficient ability:

> It was about early nontextual expositors that John Locke wrote when he asked: "[Does] it not often happen that a man of an ordinary capacity very well understands a text or a law that he reads, till he consults an

---

[1] Representatives of the united States of America, *In Congress July 4th, 1776. The unanimous Declaration of the thirteen united States of America.*

[2] A. Small and E. Downey-Small, "The American National Charter and Concept of Governance," *2010 Int'l Conf on Scientific and Social Research (CSSR), Dec. 2010, Kuala Lumpur, Malaysia.*

[3] Constitution, Article VI, Clause 2a.

> expositor, or goes to counsel; who, by the time he [has] explain[ed] them, makes the words signify either nothing at all, or what he pleases?" [4]

Constitution's Structure

The U.S. Constitution was written after a decade of American independence, operating first as independent States of America with informal cooperation in the Continental Congress, and then as the United States of America with only a Confederation Congress as the national government.[5] The Constitution was structured to provide a new form of national government for America that would more perfectly comply with the requirements specified in the 1776 Declaration.

The Constitution creates three branches of government with checks and balances on power. The three branches are defined in the first three articles: Article I, Legislature; Article II Executive; and, Article III Judiciary. There are also provisions which apply to these branches in other articles and Amendments.[6]

The Constitution gives general authority for Congress to make all laws needed for execution of powers vested in the U.S. Government by the Constitution. And, the Constitution with Amendments gives specific authority for Congress to make laws for particular Presidential employment and dismissal situations.

The Constitution also restricts the U.S. Government. The Tenth Amendment specifies the relative authority granted to the U.S. versus the State governments:

> The powers not delegated to the United States by the Constitution, nor prohibited by it to the States, are reserved to the States respectively, or to the people.

The President

The President of the United States of America is the single most powerful person in the U.S. Government. However, the President remains an employee of the People of the United States, and is bound by the Oath of Office:

> "I do solemnly swear (or affirm) that I will faithfully execute the Office of President of the United States, and will to the best of my Ability, preserve, protect and defend the Constitution of the United States." [7]

The Constitution contains numerous provisions and safeguards concerning the President. These are designed to facilitate execution of the roles of Commander in Chief and head executive of the U.S. Government, while limiting him/her to the exercise of just powers derived from the consent of the governed.

---

[4] A. Scalia and B. A. Garner, *Reading Law*, 2012

[5] Delegates of the States, *Articles of Confederation and perpetual Union...*, 1777, Ratified 1781

[6] G. Washington, et.al., Constitutional Convention Delegates, *Constitution for the United States of America*, 1787, Ratified 1788.

[7] Constitution, Article II, Section 1, Clause 8.

Purpose of this Manual

The purpose of this Manual is to provide a framework for studying and understanding the presidential employment and dismissal process described in the U.S. Constitution.

The Manual is intended to assist in locating the Constitution's provisions appropriate for particular situations which might be encountered during the employment and dismissal of the President.

Although some laws are discussed, the Manual is not intended to be a legal document or identify all laws relevant to employing and dismissing the President.

Contents and Methodology

The Manual contains Activity Diagrams and Reference & Data Tables.

The Activity Diagrams provide a picture of the presidential employment and dismissal process, and facilitate building a graphic mental framework for gaining and maintaining an understanding.

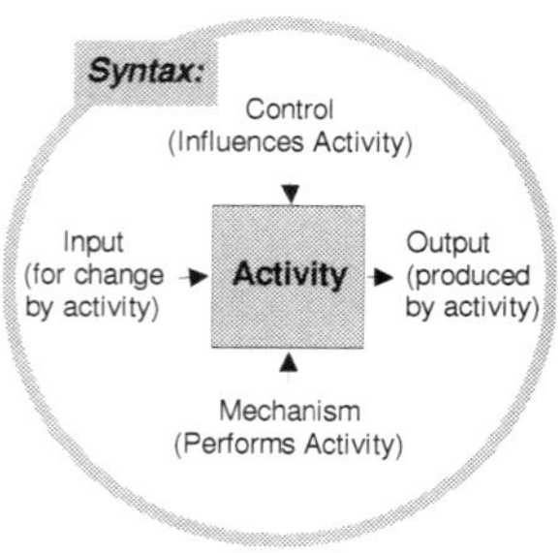

The diagrams use the process analysis language $IDEF_0$ which was derived from Structured Analysis and Design Technique.[8,9] The syntax is straight forward: Boxes represent Activities; Arrows represent Things (e.g., people, organizations, information, materials) which are produced and used by activities. The role of a Thing is indicated by the side it enters or leaves a Box: Inputs (entering left) are processed by the Activity (in box), guided by Controls (entering top) using the Mechanisms (entering bottom), to produce the Outputs (leaving right). Parentheses on an Arrow head or tail means the Things in that Arrow "tunnel" through the interface to/from the other side where, to reduce clutter, the Arrow is not shown.

The five $IDEF_0$ diagrams in this manual show: context, A-0; overall process, A0, 'Employ and Dismiss President and Vice President'; and, details of each major activity, A1, A2, and A3. To understand the process in each diagram, first note the activity/sub-activity names; then, study the interconnecting arrows.

The Reference & Data Tables provide Constitution details and references relevant to Presidential employment and dismissal; e.g., qualifications, voting stages, electoral situations, starting term situations, replacement situations during terms, and impeachment.

---

[8] U. S. Department of Commerce, National Institute of Standards and Technology, *Integrated Definition for Function Modeling (IDEF0)*. Federal Information Processing Standards Pub, FIPS PUB 183, 1993.
[9] D. T. Ross, "Structured Analysis (SA): a language for communicating ideas," *IEEE Transactions on Software Engineering, vol. SE-3*, pp. 16-34, January 1977.

II.

Employing and Dismissing the President (A0)

When the righteous increase, the people rejoice,
But when a wicked man rules, people groan.

Proverbs 29: 2 (NASB)

The Context (A00)

The overall process for employing and dismissing the President and Vice President is designated as Activity A0. Before examining the details of A0, we look at its context, shown below in Diagram A00.

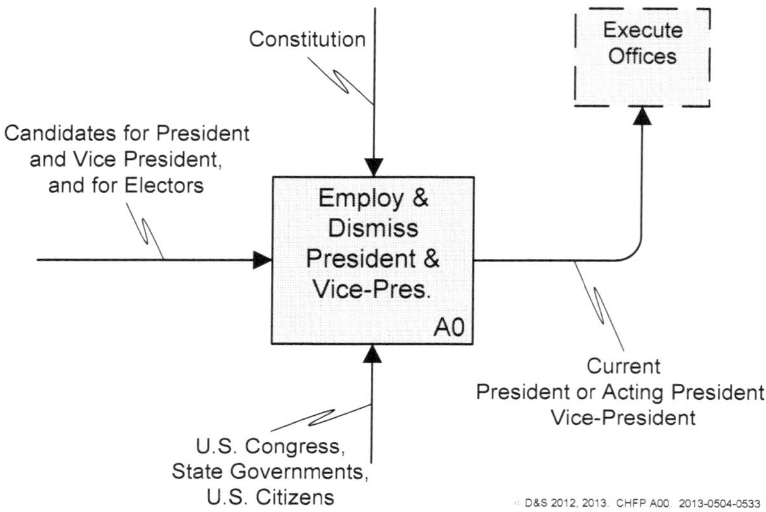

Diagram A00.
Context of Employ and Dismiss President and Vice President

In the diagram, Activity A0 is represented by the single box labeled A0. The arrow leaving the right side of A0 represents its output, Current President or Acting President, and Current Vice President.

The output from A0 serves as the mechanism for the activity Execute Offices, shown by the dashed box since its function is outside the scope of this manual.

Looking at the three arrows entering box A0, we see the following:

A0 is directed by the Constitution, the control represented by the arrow entering the top of the activity box.

A0 selects from Candidates for President and Vice President, and Candidates for Electors, inputs represented by the arrow entering the left side.

A0 is performed by the U.S. Congress, State Governments, and U.S. Citizens, the mechanisms represented by the arrow entering at the bottom.

In this manual we present the details of an activity, one level at a time. We began with the context Diagram A00 above, showing the principal external interfaces of Activity A0. Next we look at the A0 internal activities and relationships, shown in the following overall process Diagram A0. Details of each activity within A0 will be shown in succeeding diagrams in later chapters.

The Overall Process (A0)

The first level of detail within Activity A0, Employ and Dismiss the President and Vice President, is shown below in Diagram A0. This diagram displays the top level of the overall process involved. We have chosen to group the many sub-activities of A0 into three major activities, denoted A1, A2, and A3:

A1. Elect President and Vice President;
A2. Start Terms;
A3. Replace/Suspend During Term.

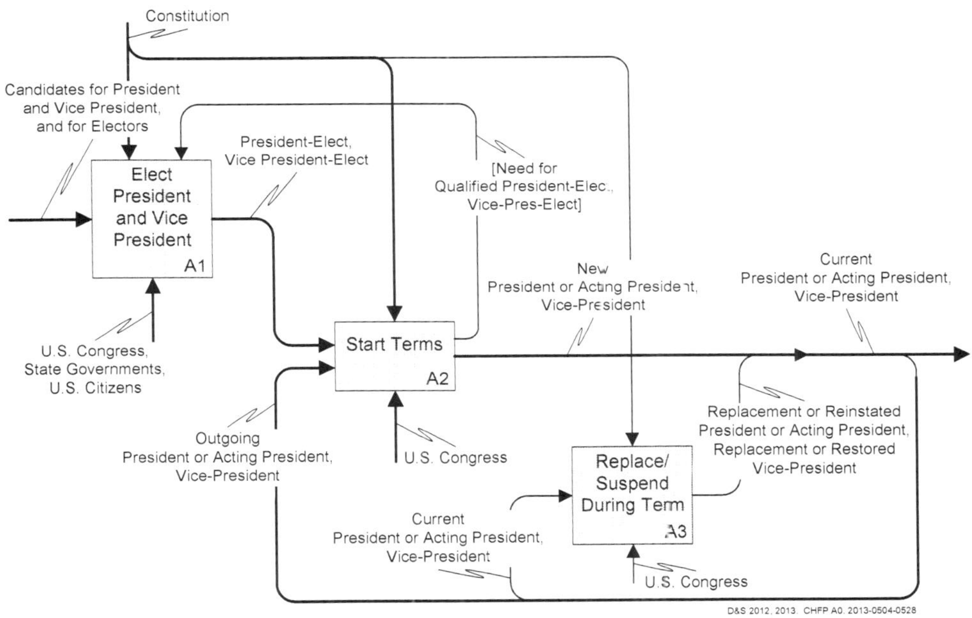

Diagram A0.
Employ and Dismiss President and Vice President

Tracing the internal interface arrows we see the first major activity, A1, Elect President and Vice President, takes in the Candidates and produces the President-Elect and Vice-President-Elect.

The President-Elect and Vice President-Elect are inputs to A2, Start Terms, where they are sworn in after end of terms of the Outgoing President and Vice President. A2 thereby provides the New President and Vice President, who are the new Current President and Vice President.

The third major activity, A3, Replace/Suspend During Terms, is activated only when one or more situations (e.g., resignation, death or removal) occur during the terms of President and Vice President. Other roles, e.g., Acting and Reinstated President, will be explained later when more detail is presented.

Election and Installation Timeline

Before examining activity details in the following Chapters, we look at the timeline for Electing and Starting Terms of President and Vice President.

The Constitution specifies timing of some events and provides for Congress to set others by law. Principal events and their dates are shown in Table II-1.

Table II-1. Election and Installation Timeline

	Roles*			Dates								
Activities & Events	Constitution	Congress	States	6 Nov 2012 **		17 Dec 2012 **		3 January	6 January			20 January
A1, ELECT PRESIDENT, VICE PRESIDENT												
States Choose Electors for President, Vice Pres. (General Election)		D	A	X								
States' Electors Give Votes for Pres., Vice Pres.		D	A			X						
(New Congress is seated; Old Vice Pres. remains)	D	A						X				
Congress Counts Electoral Votes for President, Vice President		D,A							X			
(After Count Congress Resolves any Objections)		A							XX			
(If No Majority, House Chooses President-Elect)		A							XXX			
(If No Majority, Senate Chooses Vice Pres.-Elect)		A							XXX			
A2, START TERMS												
Assess Situation; Plan Installation										XXXXXX		
Old President's & Vice President's Terms End	D	A										X
New President or Acting President Sworn In	D	A										X
New Vice President (if ready) Sworn In	D	A										X
A3, REPLACE/SUSPEND DURING TERM (not part of election and start of terms)												

Notes: * A = Actor; D = Date Setter; ** Date calculated by formula in law.

There are two State events for which Congress establishes by law formulas for setting nationwide dates: the date all States choose their Electors (General Election); and, the date all States' Electors (Electoral College) give their votes.

The Constitution set the date for end of Senators' and Representatives' Terms (Noon, January 3), and the date for end of the President's and Vice President's Terms (Noon, January 20). The Congress set by law the date for opening and counting the Electoral Votes (1 P.M., January 6).

The newly-elected Congress, with the outgoing Vice President presiding, opens and counts the Electoral Votes, and declares the President-Elect and Vice President-Elect. If no Presidential candidate has votes equaling a majority of the electors appointed, the House of Representatives immediately chooses the new President from the top two or three candidates; if no Vice Presidential candidate has the majority, the Senate chooses from the top two candidates.

The dates Congress declares the "President-Elect" and the "Vice President-Elect" cannot be set in advance since they depend upon the electoral vote outcome, as detailed in the next chapter. The declaration could be immediate, or delayed if there are objections or if the Congress must choose.

The Constitution provides for the cases where a President-Elect, due to some delay is not chosen, or has died or failed to qualify before noon, January 20. If neither President-Elect nor Vice President-Elect is available, the Constitution and implementing Law provide for an Acting President.

The status of the President-Elect and Vice President-Elect must be ascertained before January 20, to comply with the Constitution's requirements on installation. In any event, the Constitution has no provision for the Outgoing President or Vice President to remain in office past noon, January 20.

Activity Details

Diagram A0, above, displayed the overall process Activity A0 in terms of its three major groups of activities, A1, A2, and A3. The sub-activities for each group are listed in Table II-2, below. Process diagrams for A1, A2, and A3 are presented in Chapters III, IV, and V, with reference and data tables which correlate the activities, related parameters and situations, and the Constitution.

Table II-2. Activity Hierarchy

Activity ID and Name		
A0 Employ & Dismiss President and Vice President		
	A1 Elect President and Vice President	
	A11	Provide Laws for Election
	A12	Establish State's Procedures
	A13	Appoint State's Electors
	A14	Give State's Electoral Votes
	A15	Receive, Count Votes
	A16	Determine President and Vice President-Elect
	A2 Start Terms	
	A21	Provide Laws for Installation
	A22	End Terms, Relinquish Powers
	A23	Assess Situation, Plan Installation
	A24	Install President, Vice President
	A25	Install Acting President
	A26	Relieve Acting, Install President
	A3 Replace/Suspend During Term	
	A31	Provide Laws for Replacement
	A32	Permanently Replace President
	A33	Permanently Replace Vice-President
	A34	Suspend, Reinstate Self (Pres.)
	A35	Suspend, Reinstate President
	A36	Install Acting President, until Disability Removed or President Elected

III.

Election (A1)

No Person except a natural born Citizen, …
shall be eligible to the Office of President; …

Constitution Article II §1 (5)

The person having the greatest number of votes for President,
shall be the President, if such number be a majority
of the whole number of Electors appointed;

Constitution Amendment XII (3)

Election Process (A1)

Election of the President and Vice-President of the United States of America is a rigorous, multi-stage process. The Constitution specifies the process stages and gives explicit requirements for each stage. It also addresses several possible situations which might occur with the electoral vote.

The election process, designated as Activity A1, Elect President and Vice President, produces a President-Elect and Vice President-Elect. Diagram A1 shows the process composed of six sub-activities, A11–A16.

The control arrows are labeled with selected Constitutional references; more complete references are listed in Table III-1. Codes Q, V, Ep/Ev, below boxes identify relevant parameters and situations described in Tables III-2, 3, and 4.

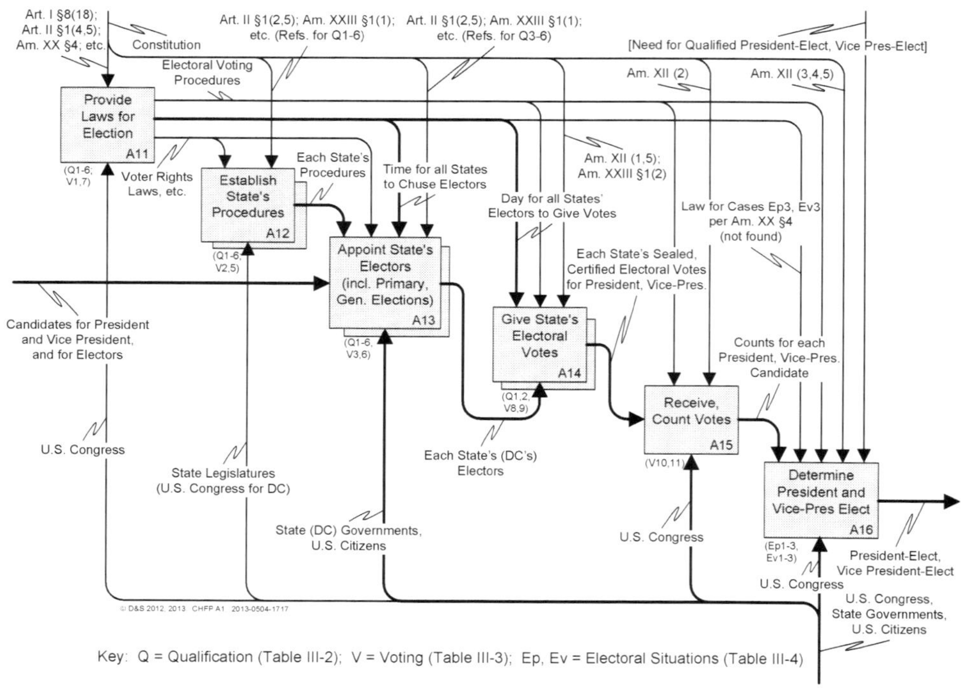

Diagram A1. Elect President and Vice President

A11. Provide Laws for Election. The Constitution gives specific authority and general authority for Congress to establish laws for elections. Specific authority is granted to enforce voter rights[10] and to establish the dates for States to choose their electors (general election) and for Electors (Electoral College) to

[10] Congress is given power to enforce voter rights by appropriate legislation; but, it is not appropriate to hinder the State's right to prevent unqualified voters. One unqualified vote in a two-candidate race cancels one qualified vote. Allowing unqualified voters nullifies qualified voters.

give their votes. Although Congress has general authority to legislate, e.g., electoral vote-count method, the Constitution's provisions require no legislation.

A12. Establish State's Procedures. The Constitution provides no detail on this activity, in which each State Legislature directs the manner of appointing its Electors (which is accomplished in Activity A13). Although the states have retained the power to develop their own procedures, they must comply with the Constitution's requirements for elections, even for cases when Congress has not provided execution laws in A11; e.g., verifying qualifications to hold Office.

A13. Appoint State's Electors. The Constitution gives little detail but several administrative procedures are provided by execution law for this activity. A13 includes many sub-activities people normally consider to constitute the election process: candidate selection, primary election, party conventions, and the general election which appoints the Electors at the time set by Congress—Tuesday next after first Monday in November (6 Nov 2012). Afterward, the news media announces unofficially the popular and electoral votes, declares the winners, and airs the candidates' speeches. Some think of these events as "the election," rather than "the appointing of Electors" who vote later in A14.

A14. Give State's Electoral Votes. This constitutes the official voting for President and Vice President by all the States' Electors (Electoral College). The Electors meet in their respective States and give their votes, on the day set by Congress—first Monday after second Wednesday in December (17 Dec 2012). Although a State's general election ballot for citizens may not allow separate votes for President and Vice President (in A13), the Constitution requires Electors vote for President on ballots distinct from their ballots for Vice President. Electors are then required to make a list of all candidates for President with their votes, and a distinct list of all candidates for Vice President with their votes, sign and certify the lists, and transmit sealed to the President of the Senate. Additional administrative procedures are provided by execution law.

A15. Receive, Count Votes. In the presence of the Senate and the House of Representatives, the President of the Senate receives and opens all States' certificates and the Electoral votes are counted. The Constitution has no further detail, but administrative procedures are provided by execution law (such as the time and date Congress opens and counts the votes—1 P.M., January 6).

A16. Determine President-Elect and Vice President-Elect. After the count of votes, the Presidential candidate receiving votes equaling a majority of Electors appointed is the President-Elect and the Vice Presidential Candidate receiving votes equaling the majority of Electors appointed is the Vice President-Elect. Execution law allows Congressional objections upon announcement of the count.

The Constitution specifies the detailed processes to be followed in the case no Presidential Candidate meets the electoral majority requirement, or no Vice Presidential Candidate meets the requirement, or neither do:

(i) For President, the House of Representatives, with a quorum consisting of a member or members from two-thirds of the states, with each state having one vote, immediately chooses by majority vote the President-Elect from among no more than three of the candidates having the highest number of electoral votes.

(ii) For Vice President, the Senate, with a quorum consisting two-thirds of the whole number of Senators, shall choose by majority vote the Vice President from the two candidates having the highest number of Electoral votes.

The Constitution further specifies that Congress may provide by law for cases where the right of choice of President belongs to the House of Representatives or the right of choice of Vice President belongs to the Senate, if one of the candidates in the group of those from which they may choose has died. However, we found no such law.

Election References & Data

The election activities described above are specified in the Constitution and in law. Table III-1, Election Activity (A1) References, below, identifies the relevant Constitution Articles and Amendments, and some of the appropriate law, for each election activity. Table III-1 also identifies Data Tables and Items relevant to each activity.

Table III-1. Election Activity (A1) References

Activity ID and Name	Data Table & Item[1]		U.S. Constitution Reference[2]		Law Ref[5]
			Constitution[3]	Amendment[4]	U.S. Code[6]
A1. Elect President and Vice President					
A11 Provide Laws for Election	III-2, III-3	Q1-6; V1,7	I§7(4); I§5(1b); I§8(18); II§1(4); VI(2)	X; XIV§5; XV§2; XIX(2); XX§4; XXIII§1(1),2; XXIV§2; XXVI§2	
A12 Establish State's Procedures	III-2, III-3	Q1-6; V2,5	II§1(2,5); VI(2)	X; XII(5); XIV§1,2,3; XV§1; XIX(1); XXII§1; XXIII§1(1); XXIV§1; XXVI§1	Voting Rights Act 1965
A13 Appoint State's Electors	III-2, III-3	Q1-6; V3,6	II§1(2,5); VI(3a)	XII(5); XIV§1(1),3; XV§1; XVII(1b); XIX(1); XXII§1; XXIII§1(1); XXIV§1; XXVI§1	3 USC Ch1 §1-6
A14 Give State's Electoral Votes	III-2, III-3	Q1,2; V8,9	II§1(5)	XII(1,5); XIV§3; XXII§1; XXIII§1(2)	3 USC Ch1 §7-11
A15 Receive, Count Votes	III-3	V10,11	I§5(1b)	XII(2)	3 USC Ch1 §12-15(a)
A16 Determine President and Vice President-Elect	III-4	Ep1-3, Ev1-3	II§1(5)	XII(3,4,5); XIV§3; XXII§1	3 USC Ch1 §15(b)-18

Notes:

[1] Data Items (e.g., particular situations) applicable to indicated activities:

A1 Activities: Ep = Electoral, President; Ev = Electoral, Vice President; Q = Qualification; V = Voting

A2 Activities: S = Start Term; Q = Qualification

A3 Activities: F = Firing; R = Replacement; Q = Qualification

[2] Constitutional provisions which specify all or part of the activity, explicitly or by logical deduction. Constitution excerpts are provided in Appendix C., Table C-1.

[3] Constitution: II§1(4) = Article II, Section 1 (Clause 4).

[4] Amendment: XX§3(2) = Amendment XX, Section 3 (Clause 2).

[5] Selected Law references for illustration; excerpts are provided in Appendices D and E, with Activity cross-references.

[6] U.S. Code: 3 USC Ch1 §19 = Title 3, United States Code, Chapter 1, Section 19. (62 Stat. 672, as amended)

Three election data tables follow:

Table III-2 Qualifications (Q);
Table III-3 Voting Steps (V);
Table III-4 Electoral Vote Situations (Ep, Ev)

Table III-2. Qualifications (Q)

ITEM	Position	Qualifications[1]	Constitutional Reference*	
			Article	Amend.
Q1	President[2]	Natural Born Citizen (or Citizen of the United States, at the time of the Adoption of this Constitution); Attained 35 years; Resident 14 years within U.S.; and, not previously breached Oath to support the U.S. Constitution, unless Congress removed disability by 2/3 vote of both houses. No one may be elected President more than twice, and no one who has been President, or acted as President, for more than two years of another person's term may be elected President more than once. A party previously impeached, convicted and removed from Office under the United States shall be disqualified.	I §3 (7); II §1 (5)	XIV §3; XXII §1
Q2	Vice-President	(Same as for President)	I §3 (7)	XII (5)
Q3	State's Electors for U.S. President and Vice-President	Must not be a U.S. Senator or Representative, or person holding office of trust or profit under the U.S., and not previously breached Oath to support the U.S. Constitution (otherwise, same as required for electors of the most numerous branch of the respective State legislatures)	II §1 (2b)	XIV §3; XVII (1b)
Q4	D.C.'s Electors for U.S. President and Vice-President	(Must not hold an office of trust or profit under the U S.[3]) Not previously breached Oath to support the U.S. Constitution.	II §1 (2b); I §8 (17)	XIV §3; XXIII §1
Q5	Voter[4]	Inhabitant of State, 18 years old, and U.S. Citizen; regardless of race, color, or previous condition of servitude; regardless of sex; but not having participated in rebellion or other crime. (May not be conditioned on payment of poll tax or other tax.)		XIV §2; XV §1; XIX §1; XXIV §1; XXVI §1
Q6	Citizen of U.S.[5] and of a State	All persons born or naturalized in the U.S., and subject to the jurisdiction thereof, are citizens of the U.S. and the State wherein they reside. (Congress shall have Power ... To establish an uniform Rule of Naturalization...)	I §8 (4)	XIV §1 (1)

Notes:

[1] Paraphrases used here; see Constitution for actual text, and Appendix C, Table C-1 for excerpts.

[2] The President needed to be only a U.S. Citizen when the Constitution was adopted; since then he/she must be a Natural Born Citizen. "The Constitution does not, in words, say who shall be natural-born citizens. ... At common-law, with the nomenclature of which the framers of the Constitution were familiar, it was never doubted that all children born in a country of parents who were its citizens became themselves, upon their birth, citizens also. These were natives, or natural-born citizens, as distinguished from aliens or foreigners." Minor v. Happersett, Supreme Court of the United States, 88 U.S. 162; 21 Wall. 162, October 1874 Term. (See distinction in Item Q6.)

[3] Article II. and Amendment XXIII do not address the requirement that no one holding an office of trust or profit under the U.S. may be an Elector for the District of Columbia (D.C.). It seems reasonable the Article II requirement also applies to D.C. Electors.

[4] A voter must be a U.S. Citizen as defined in Item Q6.

[5] A U.S. Citizen is anyone born in the U.S. (regardless of parentage) or any foreigner who has been naturalized by the uniform rule established by Congress, and subject to the jurisdiction of the U.S. Unless provided within the "uniform rule" for naturalization, the President does not have the power to grant U.S. Citizenship to aliens, regardless of any pardon or amnesty proclamation under Article II §2 (1b) to the contrary.

Table III-3. Voting Steps (V)

ITEM	Topic	Actor	Action*	Constitutional Reference: Article	Constitutional Reference: Amend.
V1	Appointing Electors for State[1]	U.S. Congress	May Determine Time of Choosing Electors.[2]	II §1 (4)	
V2		State Legislature	May Direct Manner of Appointing a number of Electors equal to the whole number of Senators and Representatives to which the State is entitled in Congress.	II §1 (2a)	
V3		State (per V1, V2 above)	Appoint Electors at Time Determined and in Manner Directed above.	II §1 (2a, 4)	
V5	Appointing Electors for D.C.	U.S. Congress	May Direct Manner of Appointing a number of Electors for President and Vice President equal to the whole number of Senators and Representatives to which the District would be entitled in Congress if the District where a State, but in no event more than the least populous State.		XXIII §1 (1)
V6		The District (D.C.)	Appoint Electors at Time Determined and in Manner Directed above.	II §1 (4)	XXIII §1
V7	Electors Voting[3]	U.S. Congress	May Determine Day on which Electors throughout the United States give their votes.[4]	II §1 (4)	
V8		Electors for State	Meet in respective states and vote by ballot for President and Vice-President, one of whom, at least, shall not be from same state with themselves; they shall name in their ballots the person voted for as President, and in distinct ballots the person voted for as Vice-President, and they shall make distinct lists of all persons voted for as President, and... Vice-President, and of the number of votes for each, which lists they shall sign and certify, and transmit sealed to the seat of government of the United States, directed to the President of the Senate.		XII (1)
V9		Electors for the District (D.C.)	Meet in the District and perform such duties as provided by the twelfth article of amendment. (i.e., vote and transmit)		XXIII §1; XII (1)
V10	Receiving and Counting Votes[5]	President of the Senate in presence of Senate and House of Representatives	Open all certificates[6]		XII (2)
V11			Count Votes for President and Vice-President[6] (The results of the votes are described in Table III-4, Electoral Situations.)		XII (2)

Notes:

* Paraphrases are used here; see Constitution for actual text, and Appendix C, Table C-1, for excerpts.

[1] See Title 3, United States Code, Chapter 1, Sections 1-6 (3 USC Ch1 §1-6).

[2] "The electors of President and Vice President shall be appointed, in each State, on the Tuesday next after the first Monday in November, in every fourth year succeeding every election of a President and Vice President." (3 USC Ch1 §1). U.S. Code excerpt from National Archives & Records Administration, www.archives.gov, downloaded Sep 11, 2012.

[3] See 3 USC Ch1 §7-11.

[4] "The electors of President and Vice President of each State shall meet and give their votes on the first Monday after the second Wednesday in December next following their appointment at such place in each State as the legislature of such State shall direct." (3 USC Ch1 §7).

[5] See 3 USC Ch1 §12-18.

[6] "Congress shall be in session on the sixth day of January succeeding every meeting of the electors. The Senate and House of Representatives shall meet in the Hall of the House of Representatives at the hour of 1 o'clock in the afternoon on that day, and the President of the Senate shall be their presiding officer. Two tellers shall be previously appointed on the part of the Senate and two on the part of the House of Representatives, to whom shall be handed, as they are opened by the President of the Senate, all the certificates and papers purporting to be certificates of the electoral votes, which certificates and papers shall be opened, presented, and acted upon in the alphabetical order of the States, beginning with the letter A; and said tellers, having then read the same in the presence and hearing of the two Houses, shall make a list of the votes as they shall appear from the said certificates; and the votes having been ascertained and counted according to the rules in this subchapter provided, the result of the same shall be delivered to the President of the Senate." (3 USC Ch1 §15(a))

Table III-4. Electoral Situations (Ep, Ev)
(after Electoral Votes Counted in Congress)

ITEM	Electoral Vote Count[1]	Action Specified[1]	Constitutional Reference	
			Article	Amend.
President				
Ep1	One person receives votes equalling majority of electors appointed.	Person having greatest number of votes for President shall be President.[2]	II §1 (5)	XII (3)
Ep2	No person receives such majority.	House immediately chooses President by ballot (majority vote, one vote per state, quorum 2/3 states) from up to three of those receiving the highest number of electoral votes.[3]	II §1 (5)	XII (3)
Ep3	No Candidate receives majority, and any person from whom House may choose a President has died.	Congress may by law provide for this case.[4]	II §1 (5)	XX §4
Vice-President				
Ev1	One person receives votes equalling majority of electors appointed.	Person having greatest number of votes for Vice-President shall be Vice-President.[2]	II §1 (5)	XII (4,5)
Ev2	No person receives such majority.	Senate shall choose Vice President (majority Senators, quorum 2/3 Senators) from the two receiving the highest number of electoral votes.[3]	II §1 (5)	XII (4,5)
Ev3	No Candidate receives majority, and any person from whom Senate may choose a Vice President has died.	Congress may by law provide for this case.[4]	II §1 (5)	XII (5); XX §4

Notes:

[1] Paraphrases used here; see Constitution for actual text; Appendix C, Table C-1, for excerpts.

[2] This provision is implemented by Title 3, U.S. Code, Chapter 1, Sections 15(b)-18 under general executuion authority specified in the Constitution Article I, Section 8 (Clause 18). Immediately after the count, "the President of the Senate ... shall thereupon announce the state of the vote, which announcement shall be deemed a sufficient declaration of the persons, if any, elected President and Vice President of the United States, and, together with a list of the votes, be entered on the Journals of the two Houses. Upon such reading of any such certificate or paper, the President of the Senate shall call for objections, if any. Every objection shall be made in writing, and shall state clearly and concisely, and without argument, the ground thereof, and shall be signed by at least one Senator and one Member of the House of Representatives before the same shall be received. When all objections so made to any vote or paper from a State shall have been received and read, ..." (3 USC Ch1 §15(b)) The code continues (3 USC Ch1 §15(c)-18), directing how the objections are to be resolved, recognizing it could take several days.

[3] This situation could result in a President-Elect or Vice President-Elect who does not have the most electoral votes.

[4] We found no such law.

IV.

Starting Terms (A2)

Before he enter on the Execution of his Office,
he shall take the following Oath or Affirmation:--
"I do solemnly swear (or affirm) that I will faithfully execute
the Office of President of the United States,
and will to the best of my Ability, preserve, protect and defend
the Constitution of the United States."

Constitution Article II §1 (8)

If a President shall not have been chosen
before the time fixed for the beginning of his term,
or if the President elect shall have failed to qualify,
then the Vice President elect shall act as President
until a President shall have qualified;

Constitution Amendment XX §3 (2)

Starting Terms Process (A2)

The start of new Presidential and Vice Presidential terms begins with the end of the predecessors' terms. The Constitution specifies the terms of President and Vice President shall end at noon January 20 in the four-year presidential cycle.

The process for starting new terms is shown in Diagram A2, Start Terms. The control arrows are labeled with selected Constitutional references; more complete references are listed in Table IV-1. The S-codes on the arrows and boxes refer to Start-Term Items defined in Table IV-2; Q-codes were defined in Table III-2.

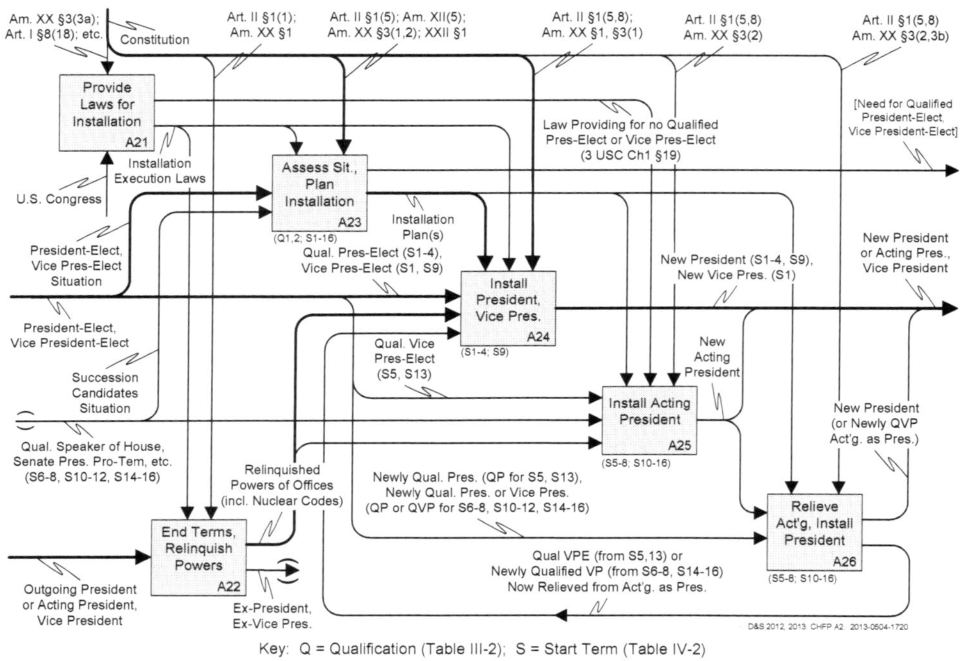

Diagram A2. Start Terms

The diagram shows Activity A2 composed of six sub-activities. Sub-Activity A22, which transforms the Outgoing President and Outgoing Vice President into Ex-President and Ex-Vice President, is normally followed by A24 which installs the President-Elect and Vice President-Elect as the New President and New Vice President, respectively. However, the process varies with the situation, which is assessed in A23.

A21. Provide Laws for Installation. The Constitution gives specific authority for Congress to provide by law for situations where neither a President-Elect or Vice President-Elect are available at the start of a new term. The Constitution also gives general authority for Congress to establish other execution laws needed to end and start terms. However, execution laws are not required so their absence does not abate the Constitution's requirements.

A22. End Terms, Relinquish Powers. This activity performs all tasks necessary to relieve Outgoing President and Vice President of the Powers of Office at the moment the terms end. The relinquished powers are transferred for use by A24 in normal situations and by A25 in situations requiring an Acting President. The Constitution gives the Ex-President and Ex-Vice-President no further roles, regardless of the situation including delay installing a President.

A23. Assess Situation, Plan Installation. This activity is required to assess the situation, prior to noon January 20, and identify the corresponding installation plan specified by the Constitution. It must ascertain if the President-Elect and Vice President-Elect have been chosen by the Congress (Activity A16 described in Chapter III), if they are alive, and if they have qualified (Table III-2, Items Q1, Q2). Activity A23 must make the determination, plan and prepare for the required installations as shown in Table IV-2, Start Term Situations.

This activity also identifies any remaining needs for qualified President and Vice President. In Items S5 and S13, the Qualified Vice President-Elect serves as Acting President "until a President shall have qualified" indicating the House of Representatives resumes work in A16 to choose a Qualified President-Elect.[11] And, in Item S6, the Acting President serves "until a President or Vice President shall have qualified" indicating both Houses must resume work in A16.

A24. Install President, Vice President. In this activity the Qualified President-Elect is installed as the New President at noon, January 20, provided the chosen President-Elect has qualified and is alive, without regard for the situation of the Vice President-Elect (S1-S4). However, if the President-Elect has died (S9), the chosen Qualified Vice President-Elect is installed as the New President.[12]

In the normal situation (S1), where both the chosen President-Elect and Vice President-Elect are qualified and alive, this activity also installs the Qualified Vice President-Elect as the New Vice President.

A25. Install Acting President. This activity handles all other cases. If the President-Elect has not been chosen or has failed to qualify (S5, S13), the Vice President-Elect is installed as Acting President until a President qualifies.[13]

However, if neither the President-Elect nor the Vice President-Elect has been chosen, has qualified, and is alive (S6-S8, S10-S12, S14-S16), Congress has

---

[11] If the President-Elect has not qualified, then, of the Candidates who have qualified, none has the majority Electoral vote. Therefore, Amendment XII (3b) would apply. (See Table III-4, Ep2.)

[12] To be "installed" as President, the Qualified President-Elect or Vice President-Elect shall first take the Oath in Article II §1 (8) and then he "enter[s] on the Execution of his Office."

[13] The wording of Amendment XX §3 (2) recognizes the States and Congress might err by voting for and declaring as President-Elect a candidate who has "failed to qualify." This would not mean the candidate is not qualified; it would mean he has failed to demonstrate he is qualified. In which case, the Amendment requires the qualified Vice President-Elect be sworn-in as Acting President. By ratifying this Amendment, at least three-fourths of the States considered Presidential Qualification so vital it must be honored without exception—even after a President is chosen.

provided a law which specifies the order of succession for installation as Acting President: the qualified Speaker of the House of Representatives; the qualified President pro tempore of the Senate; then, a specific sequence of qualified principal executive officers—beginning with Secretary of State, Secretary of the Treasury, Secretary of Defense, Attorney General, and followed by nine others.

A26. Relieve Acting, Install President. In Items S5 or S13 when a President shall have qualified, this activity relieves the Acting President (the qualified VP) and installs the New President. In S6-8, S10-S12, or S14-16 when a President shall have qualified, the Acting President is relieved and the newly Qualified President is installed as the New President. But if a Vice President qualifies first, it is deduced in Table IV-2 whether he becomes President or Acting President.

Also, a Qualified Vice President Elect (QVPE) or newly Qualified Vice President (QVP) who was serving as Acting President and is later relieved by a newly Qualified President (QP), can then be sworn-in as Vice President in A24. The associated transfers of power are included within A26.

Starting Term References & Data

The start term activities described above are specified in the Constitution and in law. Table IV-1, Start Term Activity (A2) References, identifies the relevant Articles and Amendments, and selected Law for each start term activity.

Table IV-1. Start Term Activity (A2) References

Activity ID and Name	Data Table & Item[1]		U.S. Constitution Reference[2] Constitution[3]	U.S. Constitution Reference[2] Amendment[4]	Law Ref[5] U.S. Code[6]
A2 Start Terms					
A21 Provide Laws for Installation			I§5(1b); I§7(4); I§8(18); VI(2)	X; XIV§5; XX§3(3a)	
A22 End Terms, Relinquish Powers			II§1(1)	XX§1	
A23 Assess Situation, Plan Installation	IV-2; III-2	S1-16; Q1,2	II§1(5)	XII(5); XIV§3; XX§1; XX§3(1,2); XXII§1	3 USC Ch1 §19, 20
A24 Install President, Vice President	IV-2	S1-4, S9	II§1(5,8); VI(3a)	XII(5); XIV§3; XX§1; XX§3(1)	
A25 Install Acting President	IV-2	S5-8, S10-16	II§1(5,8)	XIV§3; XX§3(2)	3 USC Ch1 §19
A26 Relieve Acting, Install President	IV-2	S5-8, S10-16	II§1(5,8)	XIV§3; XX§3(2,3b)	

Notes:

[1] Data Items (e.g., particular situations) applicable to indicated activities:
A1 Activities: Ep = Electoral, President; Ev = Electoral, Vice President; Q = Qualification; V = Voting
A2 Activities: S = Start Term; Q = Qualification
A3 Activities: F = Firing; R = Replacement; Q = Qualification

[2] Constitutional provisions which specify all or part of the activity, explicitly or by logical deduction. Constitution excerpts are provided in Appendix C., Table C-1.

[3] Constitution: II§1(4) = Article II, Section 1 (Clause 4).

[4] Amendment: XX§3(2) = Amendment XX, Section 3 (Clause 2).

[5] Selected Law references for illustration; excerpts are provided in Appendices D and E, with Activity cross-references.

[6] U.S. Code: 3 USC Ch1 §19 = Title 3, United States Code, Chapter 1, Section 19. (62 Stat. 672, as amended)

Table IV-1 also identifies relevant Start Term Situation Data Items, defined with additional references in Table IV-2. (Table IV-2 contains paraphrases; see Constitution for actual wording, and Appendix C, Table C-1 for excerpts.)

Table IV-2. Start Term Situations (S)
(Noon, January 20, when Predecessors' Terms End, Amendment XX. §1)

ITEM	Start Term Situation		Action Specified		Constitutional Reference	
	President Elect	VP Elect	President Installation[1]	Vice-President Installation[2]	Article	Amend.
S1	Qualified[3]	Qualified[3]	QPE >> P	QVPE >> VP	II §1 (8)	XX §1
S2		Has Not Qualified	QPE >> P	(Later)[4]	II §1 (8)	XX §1
S3		Dead	QPE >> P	(Later)[4]	II §1 (8)	XX §1
S4		Not Chosen	QPE >> P	(Later)[4]	II §1 (8)	XX §1
S5	Has Not Qualified[10]	Qualified	QVPE >> AP, until a President shall have qualified[8]; then QP >> P	(Later; Relieved AP >> VP)[5]	II §1 (8)	XX §3 (2)
S6		Has Not Qualified	Congress may by law provide[6] who shall act as President or manner to select, until a Pres or Vice Pres qualifies[9]	(Later)[4]		XX §3 (3)
S7		Dead	(Congress may by law provide...)[7]	(Later)[4]		
S8		Not Chosen	(Congress may by law provide...)[7]	(Later)[4]		
S9	Dead	Qualified	QVPE >> P	(Later)[4]	II §1 (8)	XX §3
S10		Has Not Qualified	(Congress may by law provide...)[7]	(Later)[4]		
S11		Dead	(Congress may by law provide...)[7]	(Later)[4]		
S12		Not Chosen	(Congress may by law provide...)[7]	(Later)[4]		
S13	Not Chosen	Qualified	QVPE >> AP, until a President shall have qualified[8]; then QP >> P	(Later; Relieved AP >> VP)[5]	II §1 (8)	XX §3 (2)
S14		Has Not Qualified	(Congress may by law provide...)[7]	(Later)[4]		
S15		Dead	(Congress may by law provide...)[7]	(Later)[4]		
S16		Not Chosen	(Congress may by law provide...)[7]	(Later)[4]		

Acronyms: AP = Acting President; P = President; PE = President Elect; QPE = Qualified Pres Elect; QVPE = Qual Vice Pres Elect; VP = Vice Pres; VPE = Vice Pres Elect

Key: "x >> y" means "x is installed as y"; "(Action)" means "Action is deduced per footnote"

Notes: [1] Before entering on execution of Office, President must take Oath/Affirmation in Article II §1(8).

[2] The Vice-President shall be bound by Oath or Affirmation to support Constitution, Article VI.

[3] Qualifications for President and Vice-President are specified in Table III-2, Qualifications.

[4] A VPE who has not qualified, dead, or not chosen (Items S2-4, S6-8, S10-12, S14-16), or is installed as the President (Item S9), cannot be installed as Vice-President; no action is specified or required until after Noon, January 20th, when the situation becomes VP Office Vacancy and filled per Amendment XXV §2, as Replacement Item R3, Table V-2, Chapter V.

[5] In Items S5 and 13, while QVPE is serving as Acting President, it may be deduced from Article I §3 (5) the office of VP would not be treated as vacant under Item R3 in Table V-2. Thus, when a President shall have qualified and is sworn in, the AP (previously the QVPE) would be relieved and could then be installed as Vice President.

[6] Title 3, United States Code, Chapter 1, Section 19 (3 USC Ch1 §19) provides for Item S6.

[7] Phrases "not chosen" and "not alive" are not the same as "has not qualified," but 3 USC Ch1 §19 treats S7-8, S10-12, S14-16 the same as S6 described in Amendment XX §3 (3). If a Qualified Vice President (QVP) is chosen before a Qualified President (QP) it is deduced: S7 and S8 effectively become S5 where QVP>>AP; S10-12 become S9 where QVP>>P; and S14-16 become S13 where QVP>>AP.

[8] "Until a President shall have qualified" implies House of Representatives must still work to choose a Qualified President (QP), deduced as described for Item Ep2 in Table III-4.

[9] The House of Representatives and Senate choose Qualified President (QP) and Qualified Vice President (QVP), respectively. Deduced by S5 if QVP chosen before QP, QVP>>AP.

[10] Deduced if later discovered President failed to qualify, powers transfer to VP as Acting Pres.

V.

Replacement (A3)

Whenever the Vice President and a majority of … the principal officers of the executive departments … transmit to the President pro tempore of the Senate and the Speaker of the House of Representatives their written declaration that the President is unable to discharge the powers and duties of his office, the Vice President shall immediately assume the powers and duties of the office as Acting President.

Constitution Amendment XXV §4 (1)

The President, Vice President and all civil Officers of the United States, shall be removed from Office on Impeachment for, and Conviction of, Treason, Bribery, or other high Crimes and Misdemeanors.

Constitution Article II §4

Replacement Process (A3)

The Current President is replaced permanently if he vacates his office (resigns, dies, or is removed), and is replaced temporarily if he becomes unable to serve. The Current Vice President is replaced permanently if he vacates his office. The Constitution makes no specific provision for replacing a Current Vice President who becomes unable to serve.

The replacement process is shown below in Diagram A3, Replace/Suspend During Term. The control arrows are labeled with selected Constitutional references; more complete references are listed in Table V-1. R and F-codes under boxes refer to removal and firing items defined in Tables V-2 and V-3; Q-codes are defined in Table III-2.

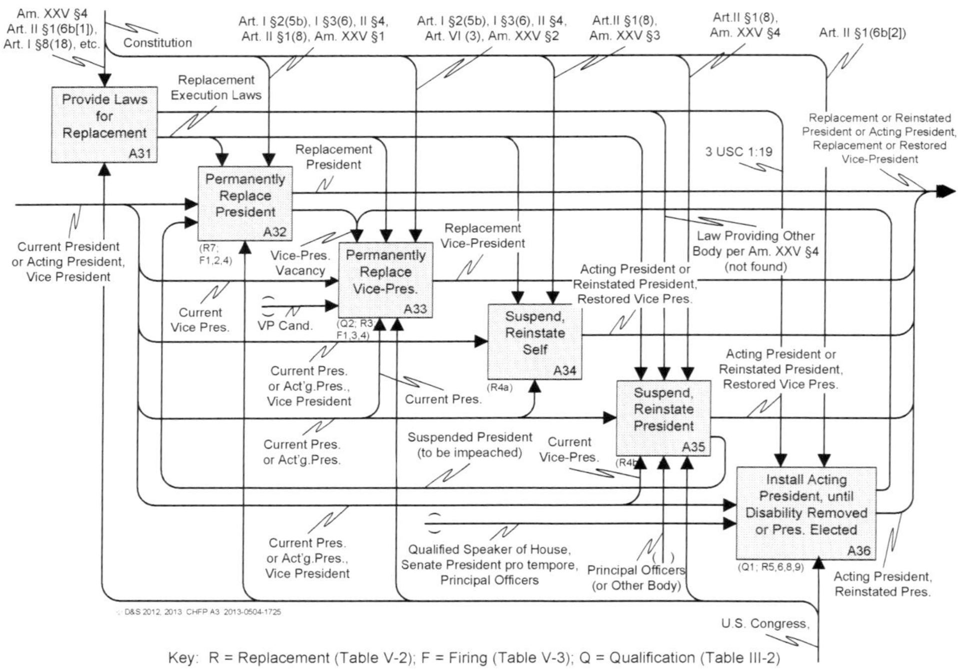

Diagram A3. Replace/Suspend During Term

The overall Activity A3 acts upon the Current President or Acting President, and Vice President, as appropriate, to provide a Replacement or Reinstated President or Acting President, and Replacement Vice President, as needed.

Activity A3 is partitioned into six sub-activities: A31 provides the laws. A32 and A33 permanently replace President and Vice President, respectively, when either of their offices alone are vacated. A34 and A35 provide respectively for voluntary and involuntary suspension of the President when unable to serve, and reinstatement when able. A36 provides for inability or vacancy in both offices.

A31. Provide Laws for Replacement. The Constitution gives specific authority for Congress by law to provide for an Acting President if both Current President and Current Vice President have vacated office or become unable to serve. Also, the Constitution gives general authority for Congress to provide other execution laws needed to implement the Constitution's provisions for replacement. However, the absence of execution laws does not abate the Constitution's requirements and each Official's individual Oath to uphold them.

A32. Permanently Replace President. If the Current President or Acting President resigns, dies or is removed from office (e.g., impeached, tried and found guilty) while the Current Vice President is able, the Current Vice President is sworn in as the Replacement President.

A33. Permanently Replace Vice President. If the Current Vice President resigns, dies or is removed from office (e.g., impeached, tried and found guilty) while the Current President is able, the Current President nominates a new Vice President who takes office after confirmation by a majority vote of both houses of Congress.

A34. Suspend, Reinstate Self. Whenever the Current President transmits to the President pro tempore of the Senate and the Speaker of the House of Representatives his written declaration of inability to serve, while the Current Vice President is able, the Vice President then serves as Acting President, until the Self-Suspended President transmits his written declaration of ability to serve, at which time he resumes duties as the Reinstated President. It seems reasonable the relieved Acting President then resumes duties as Restored Vice President.

A35. Suspend, Reinstate President. Whenever the Current Vice President and a majority of the principal officers of the executive departments (or of another body Congress may provide by law) transmit to the President pro tempore of the Senate and the Speaker of the House of Representatives their written declaration the President is unable to serve, while the Current Vice President is able, the Vice President immediately takes over the powers and duties as Acting President.

Thereafter, when the Suspended President transmits to the President pro tempore of the Senate and the Speaker of the House of Representatives his written declaration that he is able, he resumes duties as the Reinstated President, unless, within four days, the Vice President and group transmit another declaration of the President's inability to serve.

In the case a President's ability to serve is disputed, the Congress must decide the issue quickly. If the Congress is assembled when the disputing declaration is received from the Vice President and group, the Congress has only 21 days to decide by two-thirds vote in both Houses to keep the Vice President as Acting President (or if not assembled, they have 48 hours to assemble plus 21 days to vote); otherwise the Suspended President resumes duties as Reinstated President.

Although not explicitly provided, it seems reasonable: the Vice President remains Acting President during the specified Congressional decision period; and, a Suspended President could be impeached and permanently replaced (A32).

A36. Install Acting President until Disability Removed or President Elected. The Constitution specifies Congress may designate by law the Officer who shall be Acting President when both the President and Vice President have vacated their offices or become unable to serve (Table V-2, Items R5, 6, 8, 9). Congress has provided a law with the order of succession for installing another Officer as Acting President: (i) qualified Speaker of the House; (ii) qualified President pro tempore of the Senate; and, (iii) a sequence of principal executive officers.

The Acting President serves "until the Disability be removed or a President shall be elected." Next step is deduced in Table V-2. In R5 if unable President becomes able first, he is Reinstated and situation changes to R2; but, if Vice President becomes able first, he is named Acting President and situation changes to R4. In R6, if disabled President becomes able, situation changes to R3. In R8, if unable Vice President becomes able first, situation changes to R7 and he is named Replacement President, thereby further changing situation to R3.

Replacement References & Data

The replacement activities summarized above are specified in the Constitution and in law. Table V-1, Replacement Activity References, identifies applicable Articles and Amendments, and selected Law, for each activity. Table V-1 also identifies, for each activity, relevant data parameters and situations defined in Table V-2, Replacement Situations, and Table V-3, Firing Steps.

Table V-1. Replacement Activity (A3) References

Activity ID and Name	Data		U.S. Constitution Reference[2]		Law Ref[5]
	Table & Item[1]		Constitution[3]	Amendment[4]	U.S. Code[6]
A3 Replace/Suspend During Term					
A31 Provide Laws for Replacement			I§5(1b); I§7(4); I§8(18); II§1(6b1); VI(2)	X; XIV§5; XXV§4(1,2a)	
A32 Permanently Replace President	V-2, V-3	R7; F1,2,4	I§2(5b); I§3(6,7); I§5(1b); II§1(5,8); II§4	XIV§3; XXV§1	3 USC Ch1 §20
A33 Permanently Replace Vice-President	III-2, V-2, V-3	Q2; R3; F1,3,4	I§2(5b); I§3(6,7); I§5(1b); II§4; VI(3a)	XII(5); XIV§3; XXV§2	3 USC Ch1 §20
A34 Suspend, Reinstate Self (Pres.)	V-2	R4a	II§1(8)	XXV§3	
A35 Suspend, Reinstate President	V-2	R4b	II§1(8); I§5(1b)	XXV§4(1,2a,2b)	
A36 Install Acting President, until Disability Removed or President Elected	V-2, III-2	R5,6, R8,9; Q1	II§1(5,6b2,8)	XIV§3	3 USC Ch1 §19

Notes:

[1] Data Items (e.g., particular situations) applicable to indicated activities:

A1 Activities: Ep = Electoral, President; Ev = Electoral, Vice President; Q = Qualification; V = Voting

A2 Activities: S = Start Term; Q = Qualification

A3 Activities: F = Firing; R = Replacement; Q = Qualification

[2] Constitutional provisions which specify all or part of the activity, explicitly or by logical deduction. Constitution excerpts are provided in Appendix C., Table C-1.

[3] Constitution: II§1(4) = Article II, Section 1 (Clause 4).

[4] Amendment: XX§3(2) = Amendment XX, Section 3 (Clause 2).

[5] Selected Law references for illustration; excerpts are provided in Appendices D and E, with Activity cross-references.

[6] U.S. Code: 3 USC Ch1 §19 = Title 3, United States Code, Chapter 1, Section 19. (62 Stat. 672, as amended)

Table V-2. Replacement Situations—During Term (R)

ITEM	Replacement Situation: Sitting President	Replacement Situation: Sitting Vice Pres.	Action Specified[7]	Constitutional Reference: Article	Constitutional Reference: Amend.
R1	Able	Able	(None Required)		
R2		Unable[1]	(None Specified)		
R3		Vacated[2] or not filled	Whenever there is a vacancy in the Office of VP, Pres Nominates New VP; Majority House & Senate Confirm	VI (3)	XXV §2
R4a	Unable[6]	Able	Pres. Suspended by self; VP is Acting Pres, until President declares self able.	II §1 (8)	XXV §3
R4b			Pres. Suspended by VP with Majority of Principal Officers of Executive Departments (or such other body as Congress may by law provide)[3]; VP is Acting Pres, until President declares self able, unless the VP, et. al. dispute the President within time limits; Congress decides dispute by 2/3 vote of both Houses within time limits. Majorities constitute quorums.	II §1 (8); I §5 (1b)	XXV §4
R5		Unable	Congress Provides by Law for what Officer shall be Acting Pres, until disability removed or Pres elected.[4]	II §1 (6b)[5]; II §1 (8)	
R6		Vacated[2]	Congress Provides by Law for what Officer shall be Acting Pres, until disability removed or Pres elected.[4]	II §1 (6b)[5]; II §1 (8)	
R7	Vacated[2]	Able	Vice Pres. Becomes Pres.	II §1 (8)	XXV §1
R8		Unable	Congress Provides by Law for what Officer shall be Acting Pres, until disability removed or Pres elected.[4]	II §1 (6b)[5]; II §1 (8)	
R9		Vacated[2]	Congress Provides by Law for what Officer shall be Acting Pres, until disability removed or Pres elected.[4]	II §1 (6b)[5]; II §1 (8)	

Notes:

[1] The Constitution makes no provision for inability of the Vice President during term while the President is able (Item R2). It seems reasonable, if a disability were projected to be long term, Vice President would be expected to resign to allow position to be filled under Item R3.

[2] 'Vacated' means incumbent is removed, dies, or resigns. Item R3 also includes the case Office of VP not filled at start of term (Amendment XXV §3 provides for vacancy from any cause). However, Items R6-R9 in this table do not include failure to fill office of Pres and/or VP by start of terms (Article II §1 VI (6b) and Amendment XXV §1 provide only for removal, death, or resignation--not for failure to fill office by start of term or late discovery of failure to qualify so offfice is not legally filled).

[3] It appears Congress has not provided for the other body allowed by the Constitution.

[4] The specification "until ... a President shall be elected" in Article II §1 (6b), is not the same as the specification "until Expiration of the then current Presidential term" in the implementing law, 3 USC 1:19. This distinction would result in different outcomes if the next President-Elect and Vice President-Elect are not available by January 20: (i) under Constitution the Old Speaker of the House remains Acting President until next President-Elect is installed; but, (ii) under USC the Old Speaker ends term as Acting President on Jan 20, and New Speaker of House is installed as Acting President until New President-Elect or Vice-President Elect is installed. However, Article II §1 (6b1) authorizes a law to declare who shall serve, but not the period of service which is specified by the Constitution in Article II §1 (6b2).

[5] U.S. National Archives copy of Amendment XXV notes Article II §1 of the Constitution was affected by the 25th Amendment. Some unofficial copies imply all of Article II §1, Clause 6 is changed by Amendment XXV, but the provision at end of Clause 6 (which we denote "6b") is not addressed or explicitly changed by the Amendment. We conclude Article II §1 (6b) remains in effect.

[6] Inability of the President to discharge the powers and duties of his office is not defined explicitly. None is needed under Amendment XXV, Sections 3 and 4 when the President declares himself unable (R4a) or when he is declared unable in the subjective judgment of others (R4b). But if the President becomes 'unable' while the Vice President is 'unable' (R5) or has vacated office (R6), 3 USC Ch1 §19 specifies procedure for selection of Acting President, but none for deciding inability.

[7] Action Specified is paraphrased; see Constitution for actual text; Appendix C, Table C-1, for excerpts.

Table V-3. Firing Steps—Impeachment, Trial, Judgment (F)

ITEM	Firing Step	Party Charged/ Tried	Tribunal[3]	Required Vote and Result; Sentence[3,5]	Constitutional Reference: Article	Constitutional Reference: Amend.
F1	Impeachment[1,7]	President, Vice-President, all Civil Officers of U.S.[2]	House of Representatives	Party Impeached by Majority Vote; Majority constitutes Quorum.	I §2 (5b); I §5 (1b); II §4	
F2	Trial of Impeachment	President	Senate on Oath or Affirmation, Chief Justice Presiding	Party Convicted by 2/3 Vote of the Members present; Majority constitutes Quorum.	I §3 (6); I §5 (1b); III §3 (1)	
F3		Vice-President, all Civil Officers of U.S.[2]	Senate on Oath or Affirmation[4]	Party Convicted by 2/3 Vote of the Members present; Majority constitutes Quorum.	I §3 (6); I §5 (1b); III §3 (1)	
F4	Judgment upon Conviction	President, Vice-President, all Civil Officers of U.S.[2]	Senate	Mandatory Sentence--Removal from Office and Disqualification to hold and enjoy any office of honor, Trust or Profit under the United States[6]	I §3 (7); II §4	

Notes:

[1] "Impeachment, n. ... 2. An accusation or charge brought against a public officer for maladministration in his office. ..." from *American Dictionary of the English Language, Noah Webster 1828*. The President, Vice President, and all Civil Officers of the United States may be impeached for Treason, Bribery, or other high Crimes and Misdemeanors, and removed from office if convicted (Article II §4). "Treason against the United States, shall consist only in levying War against them, or adhering to their Enemies, giving them Aid and Comfort. ... The Congress shall have Power to declare the Punishment of Treason ..." (Article III §3). The terms Bribery, high Crimes, and Misdemeanors are not defined in the Constitution but left for the judgment of Congress.

[2] Deduced "Civil Officers" means Executive and Judiciary Officers--not Legislators or Military Officers.

[3] Paraphrased; see Constitution for actual wording; Appendix C, Table C-1, for excerpts.

[4] The Constitution is silent on who shall preside over an impeachment trial of the Vice President.

[5] The President has Power to grant Reprieves and Pardons for Offences against the U.S., except in Cases of Impeachment. (Article II §2 (1b)).

[6] "Judgment in cases of Impeachment shall not extend further than removal from Office, and disqualification to hold and enjoy any Office of honor, Trust or Profit under the United States; but the Party convicted shall nevertheless be liable and subject to Indictment, Trial, Judgment and Punishment, according to Law." (Article I §3 (7)). This provision allows for criminal trial after conviction for impeachment, but does not explicitly prohibit criminal arrest and proceedings against a Party while in office, particularly in cases of on-going, serious crimes.

[7] Impeachment would not apply to a person discovered after installation to have failed to qualify for office. That person would not be legally holding office, and so would not have the rights and authorities of an incumbent. Such person should immediately be relieved of title and powers of the usurped office.

VI.

Conclusion

I … beg leave to move—that henceforth prayers imploring the assistance of Heaven, and its blessing on our deliberations, be held in this Assembly every morning before we proceed to business, …

Delegate Benjamin Franklin, June 28, 1787
Speech to the Constitutional Convention

Our Constitution was made only for a moral and religious people. It is wholly inadequate to the government of any other

President John Adams, October 11, 1798
Address to the military

The *Constitution for the United States of America* is a foundational document for our civil society, written in conformance with the self-evident truths in *The unanimous Declaration of the thirteen united States of America.*

The Constitutional Convention's daily prayers for Heavenly guidance were answered. The delegates successfully labored to institute balance of powers and constraints on power, aware of its corruptive nature. The resulting document specified the most successful system of government in history.

However, as years have passed with increasing moral decline of our nation, adherence to the Constitution has been weakened. The Constitution's provisions for employment and dismissal of the President have been attacked on several fronts—often without clear understanding of the process involved.

This manual has attempted to bring together the basic elements of Presidential employment and dismissal specified in the Constitution, its Amendments, and some applicable laws, to enable readers to study and understand the process.

Epilogue

Unless the LORD builds the house, They labor in vain who build it;
Unless the LORD guards the city, The watchman keeps awake in vain.

Psalms 127:1 (NASB)

"...the propitious smiles of Heaven can never be expected on a nation
that disregards the eternal rules of order and right
which Heaven itself has ordained..."

President George Washington, April 30, 1789
First Inaugural Address

America, blessed by God, became a prosperous and powerful nation, able to bless others. But now, as we have turned increasingly against God, there are clear signs of moral and cultural, political and economic disintegration.[14]

Some national leaders responded to the disastrous attacks of September 11, 2001, by quoting Isaiah 9:10—

> "The bricks have fallen down, But we will rebuild with smooth stones; The sycamores have been cut down, But we will replace them with cedars."

—first by the Senate Majority Leader Tom Daschle in Congress the next day, September 12, 2001, and later by Senator John Edwards in a speech to the Congressional Black Caucus on the third anniversary, September 11, 2004.[15]

These leaders must not have known the dreadful context of their declaration:

> The Lord sends a message against Jacob, And it falls on Israel. And all the people know it, That is, Ephraim and the inhabitants of Samaria, Asserting in pride and in arrogance of heart:
>
> "The bricks have fallen down, But we will rebuild with smooth stones; The sycamores have been cut down, But we will replace them with cedars."
>
> Therefore the LORD raises against them adversaries from Rezin And spurs their enemies on, The Arameans on the east and the Philistines on the west; And they devour Israel with gaping jaws. In spite of all this, His anger does not turn away And His hand is still stretched out.
>
> Yet the people do not turn back to Him who struck them, Nor do they seek the LORD of hosts.[16]

America's survival may depend upon humble repentance of God's people.[17]

Our choice of president is vital, influencing and reflecting our national and individual character, and encouraging us to seek God or turn away.

President George Washington gave us timeless guidance:

> Of all the dispositions and habits which lead to political prosperity, Religion and morality are indispensable supports.
>
> In vain would that man claim the tribute of Patriotism, who should labor to subvert these great Pillars of human happiness, these firmest props of the duties of Men and Citizens.

---

[14] Erwin Lutzer, *When a Nation Forgets God*, 2010.
[15] Jonathan Cahn, *The Harbinger*, 2011.
[16] Isaiah 9:8-13, *The Holy Bible (NASB)*.
[17] Repentance must also addresses our "little" sins—see Jerry Bridges, *Respectable Sins*, 2007.

The mere Politician, equally with the pious man, ought to respect and to cherish them. A volume could not trace all their connections with private and public felicity.

Let it simply be asked where is the security for property, for reputation, for life, if the sense of religious obligation desert the oaths, which are the instruments of investigation in Courts of Justice?

And let us with caution indulge the supposition, that morality can be maintained without religion.

Whatever may be conceded to the influence of refined education on minds of peculiar structure, reason and experience both forbid us to expect that national morality can prevail in exclusion of religious principle.[18]

[18] President George Washington, September 19, 1796, Farewell Address (quoted in William Federer, *America's God and Country*, 2000).

Appendix A.

Amending the Constitution

"We the People" have reserved our right to change the Constitution by an orderly process. The process provides a peaceful method for the Citizens to exercise their right and duty to ensure the supreme Law of the Land, defined in Article VI (2a), conforms with the Self-Evident Truths in the Declaration.

The amendment process is started in either of two ways—by two-thirds vote of the Congress, or by two-thirds vote of the State Legislatures. After an amendment is proposed, it must be ratified before becoming part of the Constitution. Three-fourths vote of the States is required to ratify an amendment.

The amendment process can help protect minorities from a tyranny of the majority, as well as the majority from an over-zealous minority. Strict adherence by all—majority and minorities—to the Constitution, in conformance with the Declaration, is essential to preserve our safety and happiness.

The steps for changing the Constitution are presented in Table A-1.

Table A-1. Amendments—The Change Steps
(Article V)

<table>
<tr><th rowspan="2">Step</th><th colspan="2">Mode a.</th><th rowspan="2">OR</th><th colspan="2">Mode b.</th></tr>
<tr><th>Actor & Action</th><th>Required Vote</th><th>Actor & Action</th><th>Required Vote</th></tr>
<tr><td rowspan="4">C1</td><td colspan="5">(Either or Both Modes for Proposing Amendment(s) may be Independently Initiated.)</td></tr>
<tr><td rowspan="3">C1a. Congress Proposes Amendment(s)</td><td rowspan="3">2/3 House of Rep; and 2/3 Senate[1,2]</td><td rowspan="3">OR</td><td>C1b.(i) State Legislatures Apply to Congress for Convention</td><td>2/3 States</td></tr>
<tr><td>C1b.(ii) Congress Shall Call National Convention[3]</td><td>(Not specified)[1,4]</td></tr>
<tr><td>C1b.(iii) National Convention Proposes Amendment(s)</td><td>(Not specified)[5]</td></tr>
<tr><td>C2</td><td colspan="5">C2. Congress May Propose Amendment Ratification Mode (C3a. or C3b.), Regardless of Amendment Source (C1a. or C1b.)[1,4]</td></tr>
<tr><td>C3</td><td>C3a. State Legislatures Ratify</td><td>3/4 States</td><td>OR</td><td>C3b. State Conventions Ratify</td><td>3/4 States</td></tr>
</table>

Notes:

[1] Majorities constitute Quorums per Article I §5 (1b).

[2] Requirement for 2/3 vote of both Houses effectively mutes the requirement for Presidential approval in Article I §7 (4).

[3] Constitution does not specify the numbers or selection of delegates to the National Convention, but Congress may provide in an executing law authorized by Article I §8 (18).

[4] Deduced majority vote of House of Representatives and of Senate is sufficient. It appears Presidential approval is required per Article I §7 (4).

[5] Rules for Convention not specified in Constitution.

Contrary to popular misconception, the United States is not a democracy; it is a republic.[19] Article IV §4 (1) specifies "The United States shall guarantee to every State in this Union a Republican Form of Government…"

---

[19] "Republic, n. … a state in which the exercise of the sovereign power is lodged in representatives elected by the people. In modern usage, it differs from a democracy or democratic state, in which the people exercise the powers of sovereignty in person. …" from *American Dictionary of the English Language, Noah Webster 1828.*

Appendix B.

Activity Cross-References

Activities of the Presidential employment and dismissal process are presented in Table B-1, in hierarchical order. For each activity the matrix identifies applicable Data Tables and Items, Articles and Amendments, and selected Law References. More complete cross-references from the Constitution to Activities are provided in Appendix C, Table C-1, Constitution Cross-References.

Table B-1. Activity Cross-References

Activity ID and Name	Data Table & Item[1]		U.S. Constitution Reference[2] Constitution[3]	Amendment[4]	Law Ref[5] U.S. Code[6]
A0 Employ & Dismiss President and Vice President					
A1. Elect President and Vice President					
A11 Provide Laws for Election	III-2, III-3	Q1-6; V1,7	I§7(4); I§5(1b); I§8(18); II§1(4); VI(2)	X; XIV§5; XV§2; XIX(2); XX§4; XXIII§1(1),2; XXIV§2; XXVI§2	
A12 Establish State's Procedures	III-2, III-3	Q1-6; V2,5	II§1(2,5); VI(2)	X; XII(5); XIV§1,2,3; XV§1; XIX(1); XXII§1; XXIII§1(1); XXIV§1; XXVI§1	Voting Rights Act 1965
A13 Appoint State's Electors	III-2, III-3	Q1-6; V3,6	II§1(2,5); VI(3a)	XII(5); XIV§1(1),3; XV§1; XVII(1b); XIX(1); XXII§1; XXIII§1(1); XXIV§1;	3 USC Ch1 §1-6
A14 Give State's Electoral Votes	III-2, III-3	Q1,2; V8,9	II§1(5)	XII(1,5); XIV§3; XXII§1; XXIII§1(2)	3 USC Ch1 §7-11
A15 Receive, Count Votes	III-3	V10,11	I§5(1b)	XII(2)	3 USC Ch1 §12-15(a)
A16 Determine President and Vice President-Elect	III-4	Ep1-3, Ev1-3	II§1(5)	XII(3,4,5); XIV§3; XXII§1	3 USC Ch1 §15(b)-18
A2 Start Terms					
A21 Provide Laws for Installation			I§5(1b); I§7(4); I§8(18); VI(2)	X; XIV§5; XX§3(3a)	
A22 End Terms, Relinquish Powers			II§1(1)	XX§1	
A23 Assess Situation, Plan Installation	IV-2; III-2	S1-16; Q1,2	II§1(5)	XII(5); XIV§3; XX§1; XX§3(1,2); XXII§1	3 USC Ch1 §19, 20
A24 Install President, Vice President	IV-2	S1-4, S9	II§1(5,8); VI(3a)	XII(5); XIV§3; XX§1; XX§3(1)	
A25 Install Acting President	IV-2	S5-8, S10-16	II§1(5,8)	XIV§3; XX§3(2)	3 USC Ch1 §19
A26 Relieve Acting, Install President	IV-2	S5-8, S10-16	II§1(5,8)	XIV§3; XX§3(2,3b)	
A3 Replace/Suspend During Term					
A31 Provide Laws for Replacement			I§5(1b); I§7(4); I§8(18); II§1(6b1); VI(2)	X; XIV§5; XXV§4(1,2a)	
A32 Permanently Replace President	V-2, V-3	R7; F1,2,4	I§2(5b); I§3(6,7); I§5(1b); II§1(5,8); II§4	XIV§3; XXV§1	3 USC Ch1 §20
A33 Permanently Replace Vice-President	III-2, V-2, V-3	Q2; R3; F1,3,4	I§2(5b); I§3(6,7); I§5(1b); II§4; VI(3a)	XII(5); XIV§3; XXV§2	3 USC Ch1 §20
A34 Suspend, Reinstate Self (Pres.)	V-2	R4a	II§1(8)	XXV§3	
A35 Suspend, Reinstate President	V-2	R4b	II§1(8); I§5(1b)	XXV§4(1,2a,2b)	
A36 Install Acting President, until Disability Removed or President Elected	V-2, III-2	R5,6, R8,9; Q1	II§1(5,6b2,8)	XIV§3	3 USC Ch1 §19

Notes:

[1] Data Items (e.g., particular situations) applicable to indicated activities:

A1 Activities: Ep = Electoral, President; Ev = Electoral, Vice President; Q = Qualification; V = Voting

A2 Activities: S = Start Term; Q = Qualification

A3 Activities: F = Firing; R = Replacement; Q = Qualification

[2] Constitutional provisions which specify all or part of the activity, explicitly or by logical deduction. Constitution excerpts are provided in Appendix C., Table C-1.

[3] Constitution: II§1(4) = Article II, Section 1 (Clause 4).

[4] Amendment: XX§3(2) = Amendment XX, Section 3 (Clause 2).

[5] Selected Law references for illustration; excerpts are provided in Appendices D and E, with Activity cross-references.

[6] U.S. Code: 3 USC Ch1 §19 = Title 3, United States Code, Chapter 1, Section 19. (62 Stat. 672, as amended)

Appendix C.

Constitution Cross-References

Constitution excerpts applicable to the Presidential employment and dismissal process are presented in Table C-1, in numerical order by Constitution Articles and Amendments. Each of the Constitution's provisions is related to the Activities as indicated in the cross-reference matrix, using the following key:

"X" means the Constitution's provision EXPLICITLY specifies all or some aspect of the indicated Activity.

"D" means the Constitution's provision, by logical DEDUCTION, specifies all or some aspect of the indicated Activity.

"R" means the Constitution's provision RELATES in some way to all or some aspect of the indicated Activity; e.g., may constrain some aspect of the indicated Activity, or may apply explicitly in some circumstances.

Activity cross-references to the Data Tables, Constitution, and selected Law are shown in Appendix B, Table B-1, Activity Cross-References.

Table C-1. Constitution Cross-References (Sheet 1 of 7)

(Key: X = Explicit; D = Deduced; R = Related)

Constitution & Amendments			Activity A0, Employ & Dismiss Presiden and Vice President																	
			A1, Elect President and Vice President						A2, Start Terms						A3, Replace/Suspend During Term					
Constitution: Art. §Sec.(Clause)	Amend: No. §Sec.(Clause) {Ratif'd}	Excerpts[1]	A11 Provide Laws for Election	A12 Establish State's Procedures	A13 Appoint State's Electors	A14 Give State's Electoral Votes	A15 Receive, Count Votes	A16 Determine Pres & VP-Elect	A21 Provide Laws for Installation	A22 End Terms, Relinquish Pwrs	A23 Assess Sit., Plan Install'n	A24 Install President, Vice Pres.	A25 Install Acting President	A26 Relieve Act'g, Install Proc.	A31 Provide Laws for Replacem't	A32 Permanently Replace Pres.	A33 Permanently Replace Vice-P	A34 Suspend, Reinstate Self	A35 Suspend, Reinstate Pres.	A36 Install Act'g Pres. until …
I §2 (5a)		The House of Representatives shall chuse their Speaker and other Officers	R				R	R	R				R		R			R	R	R
I §2 (5b)		The House of Representatives … shall have the sole Power of Impeachment.													R	X	X			
I §3 (4)		The Vice President of the United States shall be President of the Senate, but shall have no Vote, unless they be equally divided.	R				R	R	R		R				R				R	R
I §3 (5)		The Senate shall chuse their other Officers, and also a President pro tempore, in the Absence of the Vice President, or when he shall exercise the Office of President of the United States.									R		R	R	R	R	R	R	R	R
I §3 (6)		The Senate shall have the sole Power to try all Impeachments. When sitting for that Purpose, they shall be on Oath or Affirmation. When the President of the United States is tried, the Chief Justice shall preside: And no Person shall be convicted without the Concurrence of two thirds of the Members present.													R	X	X			
I §3 (7)		Judgment in Cases of Impeachment shall not extend further than to removal from Office, and disqualification to hold and enjoy any Office of honor, Trust or Profit under the United States: but the Party convicted shall nevertheless be liable and subject to Indictment, Trial, Judgment and Punishment, according to Law.													R	X	X			
I §5 (1b)[2]		and a Majority of each [House] shall constitute a Quorum to do Business.	X				X	R	X	F	R	R	F	R	X	X	X		X	R
I §7 (4)[3]		Every Order, Resolution, or Vote to which the Concurrence of the Senate and House of Representatives may be necessary … shall be presented to the President of the United States; and before the Same shall take Effect, shall be approved by him, or being disapproved by him, shall be repassed by two thirds of the Senate and House of Representatives, according to the Rules and Limitations prescribed in the Case of a Bill.	X					R	X						X				R	
I §8 (4)		[The Congress shall have Power] To establish an uniform Rule of Naturalization, … throughout the United States;	R	R	R															
I §8 (17)		[The Congress shall have Power] To exercise exclusive Legislation in all Cases whatsoever, over such District (not exceeding ten Miles square) as may, by Cession of particular States, and the Acceptance of Congress, become the Seat of the Government of the United States …	R	R	R	R														
I §8 (18)		[The Congress shall have the Power] To make all Laws which shall be necessary and proper for carrying into Execution the foregoing Powers, and all other Powers vested by this Constitution in the Government of the United States, or in any Department or Officer thereof.	X	R	R	R	R	R	X	R	R	R	R	R	X	R	R	R	R	R

Table C-1. Constitution Cross-References (Sheet 2 of 7)

(Key: X = Explicit; D = Deduced; R = Related)

Constitution & Amendments			Activity A0, Employ & Dismiss President and Vice President																	
			A1, Elect President and Vice President						A2, Start Terms						A3, Replace/Suspend During Term					
Constitution: Art. §Sec.(Clause)	Amend: No. §Sec.(Clause) {Ratif'd}	Excerpts[1]	A11 Provide Laws for Election	A12 Establish State's Procedures	A13 Appoint State's Electors	A14 Give State's Electoral Votes	A15 Receive, Count Votes	A16 Determine Pres & VP-Elect	A21 Provide Laws for Installation	A22 End Terms, Relinquish Pwrs	A23 Assess Sit., Plan Install'n	A24 Install President, Vice Pres.	A25 Install Acting President	A26 Relieve Act'g, Install Pres.	A31 Provide Laws for Replacem't	A32 Permanently Replace Pres.	A33 Permanently Replace Vice-P	A34 Suspend, Reinstate Self	A35 Suspend, Reinstate Pres.	A36 Install Act'g Pres. until ...
II §1 (1)		...President ... shall hold his Office during the Term of four Years ... together with the Vice President, chosen for the same Term ...							R	X										
II §1 (2)		[President shall be elected, as follows:] Each State shall appoint, in such Manner as the Legislature thereof may direct, a Number of Electors, equal to the whole Number of Senators and Representatives to which the State may be entitled in the Congress: but no Senator or Representative, or Person holding an Office of Trust of Profit under the United States, shall be appointed an Elector.	R	X	X															
II §1 (4)		The Congress may determine the Time of chusing the Electors, and the Day on which they shall give their Votes; which Day shall be the same throughout the United States.	X	R	R	R														
II §1 (5)		No person except a natural born Citizen ... shall be eligible to the Office of President; neither shall any ... who shall not have attained the Age of thirty five Years, and been fourteen Years a Resident within the United States.	R	D	D	D		D	R		D	X	X	X	R	X				X
II §1 (6b1)[4]		and the Congress may by Law provide for the Case of Removal, Death, Resignation or Inability, both of the President and Vice President, declaring what Officer shall then act as President,													X					R
II §1 (6b2)[4]		and such Officer shall act accordingly, until the Disability be removed, or a President shall be elected.													R					X
II §1 (8)		Before he enter on the Execution of his Office, he shall take the following Oath or Affirmation:--"I do solemnly swear (or affirm) that I will faithfully execute the Office of President of the United States, and will to the best of my Ability, preserve, protect and defend the Constitution of the United States."							R		R	X	X	X	R	X	R	X	X	X
II §2 (1b)		[The President] shall have Power to grant Reprieves and Pardons for Offences against the United States, except in Cases of Impeachment.													R	R	R			
II §4		The President, Vice President and all civil Officers of the United States, shall be removed from Office on Impeachment for, and Conviction of, Treason, Bribery, or other high Crimes and Misdemeanors.													R	X	X			
III §3 (1)		Treason against the United States, shall consist only in levying War against them, or in adhering to their Enemies, giving them Aid and Comfort. No Person shall be convicted of Treason unless on the Testimony of two Witnesses to the same overt Act, or on Confession in open Court.													R	R	R			
III §3 (2)		The Congress shall have Power to declare the Punishment of Treason, but no Attainder of Treason shall work Corruption of Blood, or Forfeiture except during the Life of the Person attainted.													R	R	R			

Table C-1. Constitution Cross-References (Sheet 3 of 7)

(Key: X = Explicit; D = Deduced; R = Related)

Constitution & Amendments			Activity A0, Employ & Dismiss President and Vice President																	
			A1, Elect President and Vice President						A2, Start Terms						A3, Replace/Suspend During Term					
Constitution: Art. §Sec.(Clause)	Amend: No. §Sec.(Clause) {Ratif'd}	Excerpts[1]	A11 Provide Laws for Election	A12 Establish State's Procedures	A13 Appoint State's Electors	A14 Give State's Electoral Votes	A15 Receive, Count Votes	A16 Determine Pres & VP-Elect	A21 Provide Laws for Installation	A22 End Terms, Relinquish Pwrs	A23 Assess Sit., Plan Install'n	A24 Install President, Vice Pres.	A25 Install Acting President	A26 Relieve Act'g, Install Proc.	A31 Provide Laws for Replacem't	A32 Permanently Replace Pres.	A33 Permanently Replace Vice-P	A34 Suspend, Reinstate Self	A35 Suspend, Reinstate Pres.	A36 Install Act'g Pres. until ...
IV §2 (2)		A Person charged in any State with Treason, Felony, or other Crime, who shall flee from Justice, and be found in another State, shall on Demand of the executive Authority of the State from which he fled, be delivered up, to be removed to the State having Jurisdiction of the Crime.													R	R	R		R	
IV §4 (1)		The United States shall guarantee to every State in this Union a Republican Form of Government,	R	R	R	R		R												
V		The Congress, whenever two thirds of both Houses shall deem it necessary, shall propose Amendments to this Constitution, or, on the Application of the Legislatures of two thirds of the several States, shall call a Convention for proposing Amendments, which, in either Case, shall be valid to all Intents and Purposes, as Part of this Constitution, when ratified by the Legislatures of three fourths of the several States, or by Conventions in three fourths thereof, as the one or the other Mode of Ratification may be proposed by the Congress; Provided that ... no State, without its Consent, shall be deprived of its equal Suffrage in the Senate.	R	R	R	R	R	R	R	R	R	R	R	R	R	R	R	R	R	R
VI (2)		This Constitution, and the Laws of the United States which shall be made in Pursuance thereof; and all Treaties made, or which shall be made, under the Authority of the United States, shall be the supreme Law of the Land; and the Judges in every State shall be bound thereby, any Thing in the Constitution or Laws of any State to the Contrary notwithstanding.	X	X	R	R	R	R	X						X					
VI (3a)		The Senators and Representatives before mentioned, and the Members of the several State Legislatures, and all executive and judicial Officers, both of the United States and of the several States, shall be bound by Oath or Affirmation, to support this Constitution;	R	R	D	R	R	R	R	R	R	X	R	R	R	R	X	R	R	R
	X {1791}	The powers not delegated to the United States by the Constitution, nor prohibited by it to the States, are reserved to the States respectively, or to the people.	X	X	R	R			X						X					
	XII (1) {1804}	The Electors shall meet in their respective states and vote by ballot for President and Vice-President, one of whom, at least, shall not be an inhabitant of the same state with themselves; they shall name in their ballots the person voted for as President, and in distinct ballots the person voted for as Vice-President, and they shall make distinct lists of all persons voted for as President, and of all persons voted for as Vice-President, and of the number of votes for each, which lists they shall sign and certify, and transmit sealed to the seat of the government of the United States, directed to the President of the Senate;	F			X														

Table C-1. Constitution Cross-References (Sheet 4 of 7)

(Key: X = Explicit; D = Deduced; R = Related)

Constitution & Amendments			Activity A0, Employ & Dismiss President and Vice President																	
			A1, Elect President and Vice President						A2, Start Terms						A3, Replace/Suspend During Term					
Constitution: Art. §Sec.(Clause)	Amend: No. §Sec.(Clause) {Ratif'd}	Excerpts[1]	A11 Provide Laws for Election	A12 Establish State's Procedures	A13 Appoint State's Electors	A14 Give State's Electoral Votes	A15 Receive, Count Votes	A16 Determine Pres & VP-Elect	A21 Provide Laws for Installation	A22 End Terms, Relinquish Pwrs	A23 Assess Sit., Plan Install'n	A24 Install President, Vice Pres.	A25 Install Acting President	A26 Relieve Act'g, Install Pres.	A31 Provide Laws for Replacem't	A32 Permanently Replace Pres.	A33 Permanently Replace Vice-P	A34 Suspend, Reinstate Self	A35 Suspend, Reinstate Pres.	A36 Install Act'g Pres. until ...
	XII (2)	-- the President of the Senate shall, in the presence of the Senate and House of Representatives, open all the certificates and the votes shall then be counted;	R				X													
	XII (3)[5]	-- the person having the greatest number of votes for President, shall be the President, if such number be a majority of the whole number of Electors appointed; and if no person have such majority, then from the persons having the highest numbers not exceeding three on the list of those voted for as President, the House of Representatives shall choose immediately, by ballot, the President. But in choosing the President, the votes shall be taken by states, the representation from each state having one vote; a quorum for this purpose shall consist of a member or members from two-thirds of the states, and a majority of all the states shall be necessary to a choice.	R					X												
	XII (4)	The person having the greatest number of votes as Vice-President, shall be the Vice-President, if such number be a majority of the whole number of Electors appointed, and if no person have a majority, then from the two highest numbers on the list, the Senate shall choose the Vice-President; a quorum for the purpose shall consist of two-thirds of the whole number of Senators, and a majority of the whole number shall be necessary to a choice.	R					X												
	XII (5)	But no person constitutionally ineligible to the office of President shall be eligible to that of Vice-President of the United States.	R	D	D	D		D	R		D	X			R		X			
	XIV §1 (1, 2) {1868}	All persons born or naturalized in the United States, and subject to the jurisdiction thereof, are citizens of the United States and the State wherein they reside. No State shall make or enforce any law which shall abridge the privileges or immunities of citizens of the United States;	R	D	X	R														
	XIV §2	Representatives shall be apportioned among the several States according to their respective numbers, ... But when the right to vote at any election for the choice of electors for President and Vice-President of the United States ... is denied to any of the male inhabitants of such State, being twenty-one years of age, and citizens of the United States, or in any way abridged, except for participation in rebellion, or other crime, the basis of representation therein shall be reduced in the proportion ...	R	D	R															

Table C-1. Constitution Cross-References (Sheet 5 of 7)

(Key: X = Explicit; D = Deduced; R = Related)

Constitution & Amendments			Activity A0, Employ & Dismiss President and Vice President																	
			A1, Elect President and Vice President						A2, Start Terms						A3, Replace/Suspend During Term					
Constitution: Art. §Sec.(Clause)	Amend: No. §Sec.(Clause) {Ratif'd}	Excerpts[1]	A11 Provide Laws for Election	A12 Establish State's Procedures	A13 Appoint State's Electors	A14 Give State's Electoral Votes	A15 Receive, Count Votes	A16 Determine Pres & VP-Elect	A21 Provide Laws for Installation	A22 End Terms, Relinquish Pwrs	A23 Assess Sit., Plan Install'n	A24 Install President, Vice Pres.	A25 Install Acting President	A26 Relieve Act'g, Install Pres	A31 Provide Laws for Replacem't	A32 Permanently Replace Pres.	A33 Permanently Replace Vice-P	A34 Suspend, Reinstate Self	A35 Suspend, Reinstate Pres.	A36 Install Act'g Pres. until ...
	XIV §3	No person shall be … elector of President and Vice-President, or hold any office, civil or military, under the United States … who, having previously taken an oath, as a member of Congress, or as an officer of the United States, or as a member of any State legislature … to support the Constitution of the United States, shall have engaged in insurrection or rebellion against the same, or given aid or comfort to the enemies thereof. But Congress may by a vote of two-thirds of each House, remove such disability.	R	D	X	D		D	R		X	D	D	D	R	D	D			D
	XIV §5	The Congress shall have the power to enforce, by appropriate legislation, the provisions of this article	X	R	R				X		R	R	R	R	X	R	R			R
	XV §1 {1870}	The right of citizens of the United States to vote shall not be denied or abridged by the United States or by any State on account of race, color, or previous condition of servitude.	R	D	X															
	XV §2	The Congress shall have the power to enforce this article by appropriate legislation.	X	R	R															
	XVII (1b)	The electors in each State shall have the qualifications requisite for electors of the most numerous branch of the State legislatures.	R	R	X															
	XIX (1) {1920}	The right of citizens of the United States to vote shall not be denied or abridged by the United States or by any State on account of sex.	R	D	X															
	XIX (2)	Congress shall have power to enforce this article by appropriate legislation.	X	R	R															
	XX §1 {1933}	The terms of the President and the Vice President shall end at noon on the 20th day of January, and the terms of Senators and Representatives at noon on the 3rd day of January … and the terms of their successors shall then begin.	R				R	R	R	X	D	X			R			R	R	R
	XX §2	The Congress shall assemble at least once in every year, and such meeting shall begin at noon on the 3d day of January, unless they shall by law appoint a different day.	R				R	R	R				R		R				R	
	XX §3 (1)	If, at the time fixed for the beginning of the term of the President, the President elect shall have died, the Vice President elect shall become President.							R		D	X								
	XX §3 (2)	If a President shall not have been chosen before the time fixed for the beginning of his term, or if the President elect shall have failed to qualify, then the Vice President elect shall act as President until a President shall have qualified;	R					R	R		D	R	X	X	R	R			R	R
	XX §3 (3a)	... and the Congress may by Law provide for the case wherein neither a President elect nor a Vice President shall have qualified, declaring who shall then act as President, or the manner in which one who is to act shall be selected,							X		R		R							

Table C-1. Constitution Cross-References (Sheet 6 of 7)

(Key: X = Explicit; D = Deduced; R = Related)

Constitution & Amendments			Activity A0, Employ & Dismiss President and Vice President																	
			A1, Elect President and Vice President						A2, Start Terms						A3, Replace/Suspend During Term					
Constitution: Art. §Sec.(Clause)	Amend: No. §Sec.(Clause) {Ratif'd}	Excerpts[1]	A11 Provide Laws for Election	A12 Establish State's Procedures	A13 Appoint State's Electors	A14 Give State's Electoral Votes	A15 Receive, Count Votes	A16 Determine Pres & VP-Elect	A21 Provide Laws for Installation	A22 End Terms, Relinquish Pwrs	A23 Assess Sit., Plan Install'n	A24 Install President, Vice Pres.	A25 Install Acting President	A26 Relieve Act'g, Install Pres.	A31 Provide Laws for Replacem't	A32 Permanently Replace Pres.	A33 Permanently Replace Vice-P	A34 Suspend, Reinstate Self	A35 Suspend, Reinstate Pres.	A36 Install Act'g Pres. until ...
	XX §3 (3b)	and such person shall act accordingly until a President or Vice President shall have qualified.							R		R			X						
	XX §4	The Congress may by law provide for the case of the death of any of the persons from whom the House of Representatives may choose a President whenever the right of choice shall have devolved upon them, and for the case of the death of any of the persons from whom the Senate may choose a Vice President whenever the right of choice shall have devolved upon them.	X					R												
	XXII §1 {1951}	No person shall be elected to the office of the President more than twice, and no person who has held the office of President, or acted as President, for more than two years of a term to which some other person was elected President shall be elected to the office of President more than once...	R	X	X	X		X	R		X	R		R						
	XXIII §1 (1) {1961}	The District constituting the seat of Government of the United States shall appoint in such manner as Congress may direct: A number of electors of President and Vice President equal to the whole number of Senators and Representatives in Congress to which the District would be entitled if it were a State ... they shall be in addition to those appointed by the States, but they shall be considered, for the purposes of the election of President and Vice President, to be electors appointed by a State;	X	X	X		R													
	XXIII §1 (2)	and they shall meet in the District and perform such duties as provided by the twelfth article of amendment.	R			X	R													
	XXIII §2	... Congress shall have power to enforce this article by appropriate legislation.	X		R	R	R													
	XXIV §1 {1964}	The right of citizens of the United States to vote in any primary or other election for President or Vice President, for electors for President or Vice President ... shall not be denied or abridged by the United States or any State by reason of failure to pay poll tax or other tax.	R	D	X															
	XXIV §2	... Congress shall have power to enforce this article by appropriate legislation.	X	R	R															
	XXV §1 {1967}	In case of the removal of the President from office or of his death or resignation, the Vice President shall become President													R	X				
	XXV §2	Whenever there is a vacancy in the office of the Vice President, the President shall nominate a Vice President who shall take office upon confirmation by a majority vote of both Houses of Congress.													R		X			

Table C-1. Constitution Cross-References (Sheet 7 of 7)

(Key: X = Explicit; D = Deduced; R = Related)

Constitution & Amendments			Activity A0, Employ & Dismiss President and Vice President																	
			A1, Elect President and Vice President						A2, Start Terms						A3, Replace/Suspend During Term					
Constitution: Art. §Sec.(Clause)	Amend: No. §Sec.(Clause) {Ratif'd}	Excerpts[1]	A11 Provide Laws for Election	A12 Establish State's Procedures	A13 Appoint State's Electors	A14 Give State's Electoral Votes	A15 Receive, Count Votes	A16 Determine Pres & VP-Elect	A21 Provide Laws for Installation	A22 End Terms, Relinquish Pwrs	A23 Assess Sit., Plan Install'n	A24 Install President, Vice Pres.	A25 Install Acting President	A26 Relieve Act'g, Install Proc.	A31 Provide Laws for Replacem't	A32 Permanently Replace Pres.	A33 Permanently Replace Vice-P	A34 Suspend, Reinstate Self	A35 Suspend, Reinstate Pres.	A36 Install Act'g Pres. until ...
	XXV §3	Whenever the President transmits to the President pro tempore of the Senate and the Speaker of the House of Representatives his written declaration that he is unable to discharge ..., and until he transmits to them a written declaration to the contrary, such powers and duties shall be discharged by the Vice President as Acting President.													R			X		
	XXV §4 (1)	Whenever the Vice President and a majority of either the principal officers of the executive departments or of such other body as Congress may by law provide, transmit to the President pro tempore of the Senate and the Speaker of the House of Representatives their written declaration that the President is unable to discharge the powers and duties of his office, the Vice President shall immediately assume the powers and duties of the office as Acting President.													X				X	
	XXV §4 (2a)	Thereafter, when the President transmits to the President pro tempore of the Senate and the Speaker of the House of Representatives his written declaration that no inability exists, he shall resume the powers and duties of his office unless the Vice President and a majority ... transmit within four days ... their written declaration that the President is unable to discharge the powers and duties ...													X				X	
	XXV §4 (2b)	Thereupon, Congress shall decide the issue, ... If the Congress ... determines by two-thirds vote of both Houses that the President is unable ... the Vice President shall continue ... as Acting President; otherwise the President shall resume the powers and duties ...													R				X	
	XXVI §1 {1971}	The right of citizens of the United States, who are eighteen years of age or older, to vote shall not be denied or abridged by the United States or by any State on account of age.	R	D	X															
	XXVI §2	... Congress shall have power to enforce this article by appropriate legislation.	X	R	R															

Notes: [1] Excerpts, U.S. National Archives & Records Administration transcriptions www.archives.gov downloaded May 7, 2009.

[2] This general business quorum applies except where the Constitution requires other quorums for particular actions.

[3] A16--Presidential approval of concurrent vote to reject electoral votes under 3 USC Ch1 §15 could create conflict of interest. A35--Presidential approval of Congressional vote to continue involuntary suspension of President under Amendment XXV §4 (2b) would be a conflict of interest, but effectively moot since 2/3 vote required in both Houses.

[4] The second half of Article II, Section 1, Paragraph 6, denoted Art. II §1 (6b) in this table, starting "and the Congress may by Law provide ...", is not addressed by the 25th Amendment, and so remains in force.

[5] The part of Amendment XII (3) superseded by Amendment XX §3 (2) is not shown in this matrix.

Appendix D.

Electoral Law

Electoral Excerpts Title 3, U.S. Code, Chapter 1*	Applicable Activity

APPOINTING ELECTORS

3 USC Ch.1 §1, 2, 3, 4 A13

1. The electors of President and Vice President shall be appointed, in each State, on the Tuesday next after the first Monday in November, in every fourth year succeeding every election of a President and Vice President.

2. Whenever any State has held an election for the purpose of choosing electors, and has failed to make a choice on the day prescribed by law, the electors may be appointed on a subsequent day in such a manner as the legislature of such State may direct.

3. The number of electors shall be equal to the number of Senators and Representatives to which the several States are by law entitled at the time when the President and Vice President to be chosen come into office; except, that where no apportionment of Representatives has been made after any enumeration, at the time of choosing electors, the number of electors shall be according to the then existing apportionment of Senators and Representatives.

4. Each State may, by law, provide for the filling of any vacancies which may occur in its college of electors when such college meets to give its electoral vote.

ELECTOR APPOINTMENT CONTROVERSY

3 USC Ch.1 §5, 6 A13

5. If any State shall have provided, by laws enacted prior to the day fixed for the appointment of the electors, for its final determination of any controversy or contest concerning the appointment of all or any of the electors of such State, by judicial or other methods or procedures, and such determination shall have been made at least six days before the time fixed for the meeting of the electors, such determination made pursuant to such law so existing on said day, and made at least six days prior to said time of meeting of the electors, shall be conclusive, and shall govern in the counting of the electoral votes as provided in the Constitution, and as hereinafter regulated, so far as the ascertainment of the electors appointed by such State is concerned.

6. It shall be the duty of the executive of each State, as soon as practicable after the conclusion of the appointment of the electors in such State by the final ascertainment, under and in pursuance of the laws of such State providing for such ascertainment, to communicate by registered mail under the seal of the State

* Presidential Elections and Vacancies, 62 Stat. 672, as amended. U. S. National Archives & Records Administration, www.archives.gov. (§21, Definitions, is included with Appendix E.)

to the Archivist of the United States a certificate of such ascertainment of the electors appointed, setting forth the names of such electors and the canvass or other ascertainment under the laws of such State of the number of votes given or cast for each person for whose appointment any and all votes have been given or cast; and it shall also thereupon be the duty of the executive of each State to deliver to the electors of such State, on or before the day on which they are required by section 7 of this title to meet, six duplicate-originals of the same certificate under the seal of the State; and if there shall have been any final determination in a State in the manner provided for by law of a controversy or contest concerning the appointment of all or any of the electors of such State, it shall be the duty of the executive of such State, as soon as practicable after such determination, to communicate under the seal of the State to the Archivist of the United States a certificate of such determination in form and manner as the same shall have been made; and the certificate or certificates so received by the Archivist of the United States shall be preserved by him for one year and shall be a part of the public records of his office and shall be open to public inspection; and the Archivist of the United States at the first meeting of Congress thereafter shall transmit to the two Houses of Congress copies in full of each and every such certificate so received at the National Archives and Records Administration.

ELECTORS VOTING

3 USC Ch.1 §7, 8 A14

7. The electors of President and Vice President of each State shall meet and give their votes on the first Monday after the second Wednesday in December next following their appointment at such place in each State as the legislature of such State shall direct.

8. The electors shall vote for President and Vice President, respectively, in the manner directed by the Constitution.

ELECTORS SUBMITTING VOTING CERTIFICATES

3 USC Ch.1 §9, 10, 11 A14

9. The electors shall make and sign six certificates of all the votes given by them, each of which certificates shall contain two distinct lists, one of the votes for President and the other of the votes for Vice President, and shall annex to each of the certificates one of the lists of the electors which shall have been furnished to them by direction of the executive of the State.

10. The electors shall seal up the certificates so made by them, and certify upon each that the lists of all the votes of such State given for President, and of all the votes given for Vice President, are contained therein.

11. The electors shall dispose of the certificates so made by them and the lists attached thereto in the following manner: First. They shall forthwith forward by registered mail one of the same to the President of the Senate at the seat of

government. Second. Two of the same shall be delivered to the secretary of state of the State, one of which shall be held subject to the order of the President of the Senate, the other to be preserved by him for one year and shall be a part of the public records of his office and shall be open to public inspection. Third. On the day thereafter they shall forward by registered mail two of such certificates and lists to the Archivist of the United States at the seat of government, one of which shall be held subject to the order of the President of the Senate. The other shall be preserved by the Archivist of the United States for one year and shall be a part of the public records of his office and shall be open to public inspection. Fourth. They shall forthwith cause the other of the certificates and lists to be delivered to the judge of the district in which the electors shall have assembled.

CONGRESS RECEIVING VOTING CERTIFICATES

3 USC Ch.1 §12, 13, 14 A15

12. When no certificate of vote and list mentioned in sections 9 and 11 and of this title from any State shall have been received by the President of the Senate or by the Archivist of the United States by the fourth Wednesday in December, after the meeting of the electors shall have been held, the President of the Senate or, if he be absent from the seat of government, the Archivist of the United States shall request, by the most expeditious method available, the secretary of state of the State to send up the certificate and list lodged with him by the electors of such State; and it shall be his duty upon receipt of such request immediately to transmit same by registered mail to the President of the Senate at the seat of government.

13. When no certificates of votes from any State shall have been received at the seat of government on the fourth Wednesday in December, after the meeting of the electors shall have been held, the President of the Senate or, if he be absent from the seat of government, the Archivist of the United States shall send a special messenger to the district judge in whose custody one certificate of votes from that State has been lodged, and such judge shall forthwith transmit that list by the hand of such messenger to the seat of government.

14. Every person who, having been appointed, pursuant to section 13 of this title, to deliver the certificates of the votes of the electors to the President of the Senate, and having accepted such appointment, shall neglect to perform the services required from him, shall forfeit the sum of $1,000.

CONGRESS COUNTING VOTES & OBJECTING

3 USC Ch.1 §15 A15, A16

15. Congress shall be in session on the sixth day of January succeeding every meeting of the electors. The Senate and House of Representatives shall meet in the Hall of the House of Representatives at the hour of 1 o'clock in the afternoon on that day, and the President of the Senate shall be their presiding officer. Two

tellers shall be previously appointed on the part of the Senate and two on the part of the House of Representatives, to whom shall be handed, as they are opened by the President of the Senate, all the certificates and papers purporting to be certificates of the electoral votes, which certificates and papers shall be opened, presented, and acted upon in the alphabetical order of the States, beginning with the letter A; and said tellers, having then read the same in the presence and hearing of the two Houses, shall make a list of the votes as they shall appear from the said certificates; and the votes having been ascertained and counted according to the rules in this subchapter provided, the result of the same shall be delivered to the President of the Senate, who shall thereupon announce the state of the vote, which announcement shall be deemed a sufficient declaration of the persons, if any, elected President and Vice President of the United States, and, together with a list of the votes, be entered on the Journals of the two Houses. Upon such reading of any such certificate or paper, the President of the Senate shall call for objections, if any. Every objection shall be made in writing, and shall state clearly and concisely, and without argument, the ground thereof, and shall be signed by at least one Senator and one Member of the House of Representatives before the same shall be received. When all objections so made to any vote or paper from a State shall have been received and read, the Senate shall thereupon withdraw, and such objections shall be submitted to the Senate for its decision; and the Speaker of the House of Representatives shall, in like manner, submit such objections to the House of Representatives for its decision; and no electoral vote or votes from any State which shall have been regularly given by electors whose appointment has been lawfully certified to according to section 6 of this title from which but one return has been received shall be rejected, but the two Houses concurrently may reject the vote or votes when they agree that such vote or votes have not been so regularly given by electors whose appointment has been so certified. If more than one return or paper purporting to be a return from a State shall have been received by the President of the Senate, those votes, and those only, shall be counted which shall have been regularly given by the electors who are shown by the determination mentioned in section 5 of this title to have been appointed, if the determination in said section provided for shall have been made, or by such successors or substitutes, in case of a vacancy in the board of electors so ascertained, as have been appointed to fill such vacancy in the mode provided by the laws of the State; but in case there shall arise the question which of two or more of such State authorities determining what electors have been appointed, as mentioned in section 5 of this title, is the lawful tribunal of such State, the votes regularly given of those electors, and those only, of such State shall be counted whose title as electors the two Houses, acting separately, shall concurrently decide is supported by the decision of such State so authorized by its law; and in such case of more than one return or paper purporting to be a return from a State, if there shall have been no such determination of the question in the State aforesaid, then those votes, and those only, shall be counted which the two Houses shall concurrently decide were cast by lawful electors appointed in accordance with the laws of the State, unless the two Houses, acting separately, shall concurrently decide such votes not to be the lawful votes of the legally appointed electors of such State. But if the two Houses shall disagree in respect of the counting of such votes, then, and in that case, the votes of the electors whose appointment shall have been certified by the executive of the State, under the seal thereof, shall be counted. When the two Houses have voted, they shall immediately again meet, and the presiding officer shall then announce the decision of the questions submitted. No votes or papers from any other State shall be acted upon until the objections previously made to the votes or papers from any State shall have been finally disposed of.

CONGRESSIONAL PROCEDURE

3 USC Ch.1 §16, 17, 18 A15, A16

16. At such joint meeting of the two Houses seats shall be provided as follows: For the President of the Senate, the Speaker's chair; for the Speaker, immediately upon his left; the Senators, in the body of the Hall upon the right of the presiding officer; for the Representatives, in the body of the Hall not provided for the Senators; for the tellers, Secretary of the Senate, and Clerk of the House of Representatives, at the Clerk's desk; for the other officers of the two Houses, in front of the Clerk's desk and upon each side of the Speaker's platform. Such joint meeting shall not be dissolved until the count of electoral votes shall be completed and the result declared; and no recess shall be taken unless a question shall have arisen in regard to counting any such votes, or otherwise under this subchapter, in which case it shall be competent for either House, acting separately, in the manner herein before provided, to direct a recess of such House not beyond the next calendar day, Sunday excepted, at the hour of 10 o'clock in the forenoon. But if the counting of the electoral votes and the declaration of the result shall not have been completed before the fifth calendar day next after such first meeting of the two Houses, no further or other recess shall be taken by either House.

17. When the two Houses separate to decide upon an objection that may have been made to the counting of any electoral vote or votes from any State, or other question arising in the matter, each Senator and Representative may speak to such objection or question five minutes, and not more than once; but after such debate shall have lasted two hours it shall be the duty of the presiding officer of each House to put the main question without further debate.

18. While the two Houses shall be in meeting as provided in this chapter, the President of the Senate shall have power to preserve order; and no debate shall be allowed and no question shall be put by the presiding officer except to either House on a motion to withdraw.

Appendix E.

Vacancy Law

Vacancy Excerpts Title 3, U.S. Code, Chapter 1[*]	Applicable Activity

DUAL VACANCY—ORDER OF SUCCESSION

3 USC Ch.1 §19[**] A23, A25, A36

(a)

(1) If, by reason of death, resignation, removal from office, inability, or failure to qualify, there is neither a President nor Vice President to discharge the powers and duties of the office of President, then the Speaker of the House of Representatives shall, upon his resignation as Speaker and as Representative in Congress, act as President.

(2) The same rule shall apply in the case of the death, resignation, removal from office, or inability of an individual acting as President under this subsection.

(b) If, at the time when under subsection (a) of this section a Speaker is to begin the discharge of the powers and duties of the office of President, there is no Speaker, or the Speaker fails to qualify as Acting President, then the President pro tempore of the Senate shall, upon his resignation as President pro tempore and as Senator, act as President.

(c) An individual acting as President under subsection (a) or subsection (b) of this section shall continue to act until the expiration of the then current Presidential term, except that

(1) if his discharge of the powers and duties of the office is founded in whole or in part on the failure of both the President-elect and the Vice-President-elect to qualify, then he shall act only until a President or Vice President qualifies; and

(2) if his discharge of the powers and duties of the office is founded in whole or in part on the inability of the President or Vice President, then he shall act only until the removal of the disability of one of such individuals.

(d)

(1) If, by reason of death, resignation, removal from office, inability, or failure to qualify, there is no President pro tempore to act as President under subsection (b) of this section, then the officer of the United States who is highest on the following list, and who is not under disability to discharge the powers and duties of the office of President shall act as President: Secretary of State, Secretary of the Treasury, Secretary of Defense, Attorney General, Secretary of the Interior, Secretary of Agriculture, Secretary of Commerce, Secretary of

[*] Presidential Elections and Vacancies, 62 Stat. 672, as amended. U. S. National Archives & Records Administration, www.archives.gov.

[**] Section 19 may create confusion by providing for Article II §1 (6b) and Amendment XX §3.

Labor, Secretary of Health and Human Services, Secretary of Housing and Urban Development, Secretary of Transportation, Secretary of Energy, Secretary of Education, Secretary of Veterans Affairs.

(2) An individual acting as President under this subsection shall continue so to do until the expiration of the then current Presidential term, but not after a qualified and prior-entitled individual is able to act, except that the removal of the disability of an individual higher on the list contained in paragraph (1) of this subsection or the ability to qualify on the part of an individual higher on such list shall not terminate his service.

(3) The taking of the oath of office by an individual specified in the list in paragraph (1) of this subsection shall be held to constitute his resignation from the office by virtue of the holding of which he qualifies to act as President.

(e) Subsections (a), (b), and (d) of this section shall apply only to such officers as are eligible to the office of President under the Constitution. Subsection (d) of this section shall apply only to officers appointed, by and with the advice and consent of the Senate, prior to the time of the death, resignation, removal from office, inability, or failure to qualify, of the President pro tempore, and only to officers not under impeachment by the House of Representatives at the time the powers and duties of the office of President devolve upon them.

(f) During the period that any individual acts as President under this section, his compensation shall be at the rate then provided by law in the case of the President.

DECLINE OR RESIGN OFFICE

3 USC Ch.1 §20 A23, A32, A33

The only evidence of a refusal to accept, or of a resignation of the office of President or Vice President, shall be an instrument in writing, declaring the same, and subscribed by the person refusing to accept or resigning, as the case may be, and delivered into the office of the Secretary of State.

DEFINITIONS

3 USC Ch.1 §21

As used in this chapter the term -

(a) "State" includes the District of Columbia.

(b) "executives of each State" includes the Board of Commissioners*** of the District of Columbia.

*** The functions of the Board of Commissioners of the District of Columbia are now performed by the Mayor of the District of Columbia. (Reorganization Plan No. 3 of 1967, Section 401, 81 Stat.

Authors

A. W. Small

Albert Webster Small, born in Washington, D.C., U.S.A., received the B.S. and M.S. degrees in electrical engineering from the University of Maryland, College Park and the Ph.D. degree in aerospace engineering from the U.S. Air Force Institute of Technology, Dayton, Ohio.

Dr. Small managed systems engineering and business process improvement for 40 years. He is President of Downey & Small Associates, Inc., Kensington, Maryland, a management consulting and system engineering firm. He has led process analyses for GM, IBM, the U.S. Marines, NYSE, UBS, and Merrill Lynch. He was Director, Systems Integration, SRS Technologies-Washington. While serving in the U.S. Air Force he was Chief, Airborne Software Research, Air Force Avionics Laboratory; and, Director, Computer Resources Development, Policy and Planning, Air Force Systems Command.

E. A. Downey-Small

Elizabeth Ann Downey-Small, born in Leigh-on-Sea, Essex, England, U.K., received the B.A. degree in sociology with honors from the University of London, England, and a postgraduate certificate in social work from the University of Edinburgh, Scotland.

Ms Downey-Small has 30 years experience in general management and consulting. She is Vice President of Downey & Small Associates, Inc., Kensington, Maryland, a management consulting and system engineering firm. She led analysis of emergency preparedness responsibilities of 33 Federal agencies for the Federal Emergency Management Agency. She consulted to General Motors, the U.S. Marines, New York Stock Exchange, Union Bank of Switzerland, and Merrill Lynch, and participated in training courses for senior executives. She served as a member of the Steering Committee of the Society for Enterprise Engineering.

2013-05-15 DS-SOM-CHFP v.1.6 Printed in U.S.A.

19421135R00043

Made in the USA
Charleston, SC
22 May 2013